LIBERAL LOSERS

KAREN KELLOCK PH.D.

Manual for
Superior Men

A complete theory based on Einstein physics, Political Psychology, Systems Theory and Archetypal Psychiatry.

FORMULA
All success attraction
All disease obstruction
All recovery elimination

You must fast on all three

OBSTRUCTIONS:
People
Habit
Food

LIBERAL LOSERS

Frenemies who sow discord: a malicious heart hides behind loving lips. The strong have restraint, the weak do not. The problem is: surrounded by evil you just feel nuts. By smooth words/flattering speech they deceive the hearts of the simple. The enemy sows discord and division to the dumbed down who can't discern truly good from evil. You're not even supposed to reason with a fool, yet these simpletons are your enemy's army against you.

LIBERAL LOSERS

RESISTANCE MARKS GENIUS
DIMINISHING SELF-PERSPECTIVE
GREATNESS IN SUBTLETY
JEZEBEL GOSSIP
NASTINESS TO NOVELTY
WITCHES ARE OFFICIOUS
FEMALE PECKING ORDERS
JEZEBELS ARE UNDERHANDED
MINE THE PAST FOR GEMS, THAT'S ALL
MIMICKING MOM/FIGHTING THE THRONG
NARCISSISTS DO NOT CARE
MORE ALONE, MORE SUCCESS
HOME IS ALL
POST TRAUMATIC STRESS
UPWARD PATH & REMORSE LOOKING BACK
CONSPIRACY AGAINST PRIVACY
THE EMPTY NARCISSIST GENIUS
FAKE RED PILL GUYS
CONTRADICTIONS AND SOUL TIES
IT'S WHO YOU FOLLOW
BETRAYAL TRAUMA
PAIN IN THE SOLAR PLEXUS
WHAT PEOPLE ARE LIKE
LIBERAL TYRANNY
HOLLYWOOD: EVILS OF AMERICA
DEALING WITH CENSORSHIP
NASTY RESPONSES TO NOVELTY
HOME IS HEAVEN
IF THEY DON'T GET IT, TOUGH
SHADOW PROJECTSION
SCAPEGOAT MECHANISMS
HE WANTS TOTAL CONTROL
NARCISSISTS ARE PSYCHOPATHS
ALWAYS SEE THE SYSTEM
DO THEY HATE WOMEN?
SOCIAL CHARM

LIBERAL LOSERS

HE TURNED EVERYTHING AROUND
LACK OF EMPATHY
PEOPLE ON THE PROPERTY
BEING HATED
DISCARDING AND HOOVERING
LET THE FANTASY DIE
DIGNITY AND BOUNDARIES IS EVERYTHING
IT'S STILL PERVERSE
BE READY TO SET BOUNDARIES/WALK AWAY
BUSTING BOUNDARIES IS FIRST
FRENEMIES WHO SOW DISCORD
THE NARCISSIST ENVIES YOU
YOU SHOULDN'T EVEN EXIST
SELF-ABANDONMENT IS STAYING QUIET
KEY TO JOY: RECOGNIZE NARCISSIST SYSTEMS
THE BROKEN LOVE NARISSISTS
BOUNDARIES AND LOST HEDGES OF PROTECTION
TAKE A DEFENSIVE STANCE
DISORDERLY MESSERS
IT'S ALL PROJECTION
IT'S ALWAYS OP-TRUTH
ALONE IS BRIGHT, A CROWD'S A BLIGHT
JEZEBEL SPIRIT AND CRYING JAGS
THE POINT OF RELIGION IS RELATIONSHIP
MASTERING FEAR AND LONELINESS
LET EM IN: LETHAL DANGER
INTERLOPERS AND IMPOSERS
SAINT COUPLES
ABHORRENCE OF OUR SIN BRINGS FREEDOM
FRUITFUL REVERIES
WORKING THRU TRAUMA IS A PROCESS WITH AN END
WRITE THE TRUTH NOT WHAT "SELLS"
BRACE FOR CULTURAL DECLINE
ACADEMIC CREDITS FOR MORAL VIRTUE
NOT YOUNG AGAIN
WOMEN BLOCK FEMALE SUCCESS
HOW CAN YOU WALK TOGETHER

LIBERAL LOSERS

THE WEST IS THE SEAT OF LIBERTY
FROM CALIFORNIA CHAOS TO DECENCY
MARXIST PROFESSORS AND FEMINIST HATERS
JOHN THE BAPTIST WAS A SIN HATER
SOCIAL HYPNOTISM IN SYSTEMS
UNBRIDLED HEDONISM
CULTURAL MASOCHISM
FLUSH EM OUT
NEPOTISM AND AGREEING WITH WRONG
FEMINISTS ARE NO FRIENDS
COMPLACENCY AND AGING
DEPENDENCE-INDEPENDENCE CYCLES
TEST OF LIFE
SOCIAL HYPNOTISM AND REJECTION
QUESTION YOUR ATTRACTIONS!
LIBERAL CREEP AND GLOBALISM
DIVERSOCRACY MADNESS
HOW STABLE MIDDLE AMERICA WAS
THEIR OWN PEOPLE
APPEASEMENT NEVER WORKS
"REVISED CURRICULUMS"
RACIAL ESSENTIALISTS
HIX POLITIX
MORE GUNS LESS CRIME
ARNOLD EHRET FOREVER
FOOD AND WHERE IT'S AT NOW
HAPPY WHEN I'M NOT EATING
THE HUMAN OMNIVORE
MINI-FASTING ROUTINE IN TRAUMA
PIZZA DAY THEN BACK TO CORNUCOPIA
HEALTH UPDATES
END OF A LONG JOURNEY
AT THE TOP OF MY GAME
BULLY-PROOF IS HARD WORK
BARREN LAND WITH NO LOVE
THE WAR WAS YOUR STEPPING STONE

LIBERAL LOSERS

Rejection breaks down boundaries and morals, putting the personality in retrograde for now.

With rejection her spirt went retrograde showing the worst characteristics of her ancestry.

With emotional security her spirit showed the BEST of her ancestry, that's how it worked see.

A woman can be hurt badly by men before she knows better, swimming in muddy waters.

The man is the foundation of the home but the woman is the glue holding it together alone.

Women are smarter in areas in which men are weak. They play these to the hilt, believe me.

It was CALUMNY. Sure I was wrong but did she have to shout it from the rooftops? Always.

She was bored when he was in love but fell deeply--never giving up--when he'd had enough.

Rejection triggers early trauma so love addicts hold on tighter as an attempted corrective.

Had he stayed in love I woulda been bored with him but the rejection triggered longing for the bum.

RESISTANCE MARKS GENIUS

There were words in that conversation challenging your values, eroding your confidence too.

If everyone disagrees, you could be a genius. The sign of a discoverer is constant resistance.

LIBERAL LOSERS

A malicious heart hides behind loving lips. Of all advice in the world that's the one to give.

Firstly I wasn't aware that I wasn't aware, and I wanted what I wanted and it didn't matter.

That pain tunnel is the core of addiction. Early trauma is reflected in what we tolerate now son.

The whole structure is held in place by the critical parent inside saying this abuse is ok.

The pain tunnel causes one to seek nurturance from the same betrayal source: dangerous.

She was a destructive Jezebel but I wanted her approval to be social and went to hell.

Abusers come bearing gifts/flattering to uplift. They don't come with horns they just SWITCH.

As his bad language seeps in to break her soul she becomes addicted to his voice: oh!

LET: Language, Energy and Treatment is how you vet a man, so don't "fall" but think/plan.

DIMINISHING SELF-PERSPECTIVE

Satan's clever, diminishing self-perspective and emptying your self-esteem with his words.

After that onslaught you're addicted to it now and keep going back for more though it lowers.

The point of poetry is incisiveness: cutting like a sword before they've a chance to argue with it.

Dictators hate poets being incisive, a most powerful device before they can argue with it.

LIBERAL LOSERS

God said to avoid futile, useless debate so don't go there again or for you it'll be bad fate.

The lack of civility in normal discourse is enough to make any artist escape so do it fast.

No gentle genius should be insulted in groups--superior man won't be dishonored too.

They lack self-awareness and don't know what they're talking about but are "intellectuals".

Don't think back to when you had no boundaries. It's too sad and those were younger days.

If your self-perspective is 100% and then you must adapt and it becomes 20%, it's tragic.

Life and death in the power of the tongue. Words are spiritual containers of bad intentions.

A malicious heart hides behind loving lips. You know this but you still love the witch.

Keeping [an already traumatized woman] a secret is compounding the trauma, degraded.

Don't hanker over the past by inviting old friends back cuz it's never the same, that's a fact.

GREATNESS IN SUBTLETY

Your greatness lies in subtlety but that's also why they miss the depth/profundity of what you say.

It's a gross generation so subtlety's not their thing but don't degrade for those Philistines.

You don't have to prove it to them, their memory will know you're different/that's how it works.

LIBERAL LOSERS

The social hypnosis of women is shallow: one gets divorced and others in the group follow.

The girls encourage "getting more money outa him" in divorce then the judge gives her far less.

The best advice for women is to ignore the words of feminist friends or the result is ruin.

In the girl's club they build each other up saying "he's not good enough for you" and such.

"You don't have to lose weight, the man who deserves you will see past all that" they will say.

I don't see how a man can stand a woman with all her friends blabbing against him.

Her feminist friends are anti-male/pro-female and that matrix never changes without fail.

She tears down her own home--depriving kids and pets of same--cuza what her friends say.

Carefully vet friends cuz we easily take advice from them and it often means certain ruin.

JEZEBEL GOSSIP

She tells them what he said, they react. She tells him what they said, his reality goes black.

Never trust a Jezebel bringing dark gossip from her friends against you. NEVER you fool.

First she loves you then she calls you a fraud because her friends did. Drop the witch.

It's hard advising women not to have friends but that's what I'm saying: be alone, amen.

LIBERAL LOSERS

There's nothing wrong with dressing him in a certain way but everything must have her ok.

Women judge everything. When I first arrived in that small town Jezebels mocked the queen.

They judge, mock and deride then get on the horn to make sure friends do too, even cry.

Women are narrow-minded and socially-driven and to a budding new relationship it means ruin.

Feminist friends are often divorced and lonely so misery loves company: ignore them totally.

NASTINESS TO NOVELTY

Women don't know how to think and so their reactions to novelty are nasty, off point, cruel.

Of course not all women--it's a bell-shaped curve. But it's a hard science, statistics are hers.

Women control each other's views. I recall the treachery so well as I was attacked too.

The devil in them hates Christ in you, transcending this world to principalities and powers.

I unsubbed from every group because I will not adapt to lowminds and their words so cruel.

Men entertain differences not viciously attack as I've witnessed the witches when in the ditches.

WITCHES ARE OFFICIOUS

And thus the witches are officious--always nosing in where they don't belong, a nuisance.

LIBERAL LOSERS

Every time I took her [his] advice and not my own it cost me plenty and ruined my rep see.

First they love you then they talk to a friend and they hate you and go to war against you.

The only way to deal with the grapevine is drop everyone in it and go totally within.

In female community it's the Dunning-Kruger Effect of a buncha blind dummies leading the elect.

The female community is a massive obstruction to female genius: must make a choice.

The jealous Jezebels ridiculed my looks/the way I walked, anything and they'd be cackling.

They're without lines the way they'll do anything to keep YOU in line with them on top, aye.

Angry at husband they screw him in divorce as friends egg her on to get even more from him.

They get back at men--any man--for centuries of being put down tho' they had the crown.

After divorce nothing matches and he shows up with holes in his pants, that's the stats.

FEMALE PECKING ORDERS

Older sister wives beat up new ones as pecking order must be enforced: that's the hens.

Women incite riots with neighbors revealing all of your confidences just for the heck of it.

Women jealous of best friends, subtly needling them and goading them into sin and ruin.

LIBERAL LOSERS

Women flirting with their best friend's mate just to put them in their place and win the race.

Now you can see why I'm sensitive to ridicule: I see thru fools/that brings hate from shrews.

She wants things EVEN and the only way is to get an army of her friends against you, ok?

I do better in a soap discussion group like B & B cuz it's all psychological fantasy anyway.

JEZEBELS ARE UNDERHANDED

I didn't dare leave her alone with him, there's something in her treacherous with men.

I didn't dare introduce her to any friends cuz she'd get on the horn and run me down to them.

It's just a sister thing to screw each other one way or another and call it love or whatever.

Men don't wanna fight with women so instead of standing up for themselves they cave in.

She weeds out his friends from the beginning, telling him who he can see like a queen.

Life is meant to be lived, first. Then as a sage it's to be MINED for gems, like a wisdom-thirst.

Looking out the window I see 1985, 1996, 2008 in a whole new light and I'm high as a kite.

MINE THE PAST FOR GEMS, THAT'S ALL

Bible says He forgets it all--tho' we know he could recall--cuz He's true to His word that's all.

LIBERAL LOSERS

God remembers it no more, though He could, of course! He said He wouldn't/no remorse.

I don't need to recall all that to keep me good--God made me good in his divine parenthood.

Now I prepare to sail off to eternity leaving all this crap and frenemies behind, just God and me.

Don't fret over the past, mine it for gems instead and you'll see it all differently, what a blast.

Looking out the window in quiet reverie is far more productive than another movie.

The Cinderella Syndrome of three women against one is what made me this way, battle won.

Say goodbye to all your opportunities/breaks, you shouldn't have been born so privileged.

It's not the END it's the Beginning of the End--my highest blend, top of my game amen.

My life was driven by a vision, I held it in my trembling hand no matter what was happening.

There's only one way I could ever win out over those three broads: I outlived em, that's all.

Life goes on as the generations go out together. Separate while you still can, explore.

MIMICKING MOM/FIGHTING THE THRONG

The older lady said: Ok I mimicked mom all my life but now I'm free and sweet so forget it see.

I hear people yelling at me and it's women, their social devices and violence always unmentioned.

LIBERAL LOSERS

Though you could live many more decades you reach a mental point prepared to leave today.

There's nothing worse than ruled by three women since they're both crazy and collusive.

It was my ghost town era, an inner journey of fertile anarchy but appearing as a dry period.

I had to get away from the group dynamics/TYRANNY because people think they own you see.

They think they've a right to wake you at midnight to fix em a meal cuz they always take a mile.

He SAID He'd remember it no more so He makes us white as snow and removes the horror.

Tho' I fell God restored me whole that's all I need to know. Sail on ahead, God's at the bow.

It's not that they treated you badly, they treat everyone that way but you were unprotected see.

When poor I was ignored, now rich they all wanna be my friend to know, that's how it goes.

I hate nobody but everybody so stop calling me a hater and bigot I'm just a realist buddy.

I ended in a ghost town for 26 years. Long story short God put me on the Potter's Wheel to here.

Not only did they shame me publicly they made everyone hate/incited riots against me.

Tho' the sick system is long gone the experience gave me fire despite digestive issues, a bummer.

I'd far rather live in a dusty ghost town then live with misjudgment of those you're around.

LIBERAL LOSERS

Women use a sheriff as their sidekick getting back in pure vindictiveness, taking his guns/rep.

Single/eccentric women went to the camps too, solely on the gossip of neighbors--nothing new.

NARCISSISTS DO NOT CARE

We all live two lives. The one we learn from and the one we live after that. Don Bongino

Thru schools, indoctrinate em. Thru media, spoon-feed em. Increase debt, then tax em.

After all the evil deeds of the Clintons the point is the women loved Hillary/some STILL DO.

He will never care about you, it's all about him. That alone is all you need to know my friend.

Don't expect any sympathy from him--no matter what's happened you're not in his vision.

The two women were in collusion and had only vengeance [against you] in their vision.

No amount of talent or creativity will interest him since it's all about him and HIS attributes friend.

Never cower before the face of evil. Think about the times you caved in to intimidating people.

MORE ALONE, MORE SUCCESS

The more people you reject the more you'll have success for people are obstruction miss.

If girls just want bad boys that means there's no more good girls--it's guilt by association ok.

LIBERAL LOSERS

A hypersensitive processes info so fast a social occasion's a confusing blast he avoids, alas.

Why desire bad boys? Don't you want home, stability, happiness and trust all your days?

Blended families sexually connected: no lines, falling, crawling back for help "cuz we're family".

HOME IS ALL

They just assumed I was bored and lonely way out there so they'd come over, bummer!

Young love is about passion, old love is about accommodation--I just wanna be alone hon'.

Two weeks cleaning woodwork. Details keep home perfect but how many women are into it?

A whole new universe alights when getting into details: Perfectly clean walls, orderly drawers ok.

All I want is HOME and so housekeeping is my thing alone and how that star is shone, oh!

She was a masochist in those days, having morals and boundaries torn down thru trauma ok.

POST TRAUMATIC STRESS

In my period of affliction I went dead as it was happening and only now am I awakening.

All I could do was shut my eyes and endure it, I had to get thru it guided by a vision beyond it.

Do it while you still can. Human beings age and die so you gotta do it now, a flower opening man.

LIBERAL LOSERS

The problem is, while your flower is opening your friends/family block it from happening.

If self-expression [WELLING UP] is blocked the energy BLOATS at the waist, hips and thighs.

Chance: If apes learned a task the apes on the next island learned it too: I'm astonished!

Just when I want room to think, that's when they want my attention: that's the system.

The kids are violent, stay away from them dammit. Even the slightest threat, REJECT it!

The more I was alone [free of their chaos] the more they'd come around bothering the boss.

Adapt to them, utter failure. Eject them, do your own thing and the whole world's your oyster.

Things started bad but now they're good. Don't wallow in memory but enjoy your new lifeblood.

So you had to go thru all that to get to here. Enjoy where you are, don't waste it on tears.

UPWARD PATH & REMORSE LOOKING BACK

2 life phases: overcoming and success [enjoying]. The first is hell, the latter is celebrating.

The Hero's Path ain't all roses and accolades. It's hell in spades/torture to make you great.

Being on the Potter's Wheel isn't all gentle nudging, it can be frightening like a boot camp setting.

I learned from my violent invaders all I need to know about human nature, thank you Father.

LIBERAL LOSERS

Life is an evolution, an uphill path or a downward one depending on the road, wide or narrow.

Wide path is the one everyone's on. Avoid it like the plague though they'll call you odd hon'.

The narrow path is holy and separate, a hideous stigma to the elect who don't know about it.

There is no past just a buncha vaporous interactions that with death are forever forgotten.

You could be yourself around him/her but not around him/her, that explains your neurosis dear.

I did wrong but repented so why give you a chance to judge me more? Don't count on it.

The new generations are guilty of people-worship but without God they're all fullashit.

At this phase I don't have to put up with how you react to what I say, I know enough to insulate.

Crisis is ever an opportunity for these people. They always consolidate to further an agenda.

A senile old codger doing nothing but promoting radicalism and instability around the world.

CONSPIRACY AGAINST PRIVACY

Alone in wilderness I was totally prolific and busy as a lunatic but they assumed I was a wreck.

They would not leave me alone, the more I wanted solitude—a cultural conspiracy to be rude.

It was like they were jealous of my privacy and the fact I was most happy without company.

LIBERAL LOSERS

They called me rude for not letting em in but I called em rude for invading my privacy, amen.

Introverts can feel this constant pull to be social more than those part of the mazeway/phones.

False churches are especially threatened by your solitude, you're supposed to be social dude.

I let em hook up on the land and what did I get in return? Arrogant superiority of liberals.

So I let em hook up on the land and what did I get in return? Them bringing all their friends.

Their brother, lover, neighbor, acquaintances from the bar. All their stuff and thoughts galore.

I just gave em a hookup that was it but the pagans always wanna impose their bagashit.

They just can't help themselves from imposing since their superior view is obvious isn't it?

Tho' I was the giver they asked me to go to their rituals and I kept having to defend why "NO!"

Ellen on being "kind". See what I mean about the two sides of virtue signalers? Oh my.

THE EMPTY NARCISSIST GENIUS

The narcissist does not appreciate his own existence, only feedback about his own existence.

I get no feedback, that trained me to be satisfied with the invisible God who wrote it in fact.

Where a human being shoulda been there's a black hole consuming everything around.

LIBERAL LOSERS

How could an empty void, a person who doesn't exist, an absence turn out to be a great genius?

The dichotomy between narcissist image and inner reality is the "mask of sanity" in psychology.

Narcissistic injury is a challenge to his grandiosity, mortification a challenge to his false self.

What they want: SSS. Secondary narcissistic supply, sex and services--that's the extent of it.

The cops are retiring, the criminals are out of prison and they wanna take your guns son.

When you hear the word "carbon footprint" you've heard the Luciferian word for DESTRUCT.

It's a wide path to hell and just a trickle to heaven so why waste time thinking about them?

The news isn't positive just cuz you want it that way. Do you want truth or to blindly look away?

FAKE RED PILL GUYS

He fancies himself a red pill guy but won't believe truth till he hears it on the news, oh my.

It's an insult to know him and the sooner you realize that the sooner you'll have success hon'.

It was an insult to know him but that soul tie of sexual chemistry kept you down in the ring.

You want to tell him everything but honey he couldn't care less what you think--see reality.

He says to "stay positive" while the roof falls in. I can see now he's steeped in liberalism.

LIBERAL LOSERS

It's an insult to know him since you're competing with his fans, a Dunning-Kruger Effect.

A narcissist without an inner core has "seen the light" but his talks are boring, slow and trite.

They win by controlling the narrative--language, definitions, framing--then bashing us for it.

It's so ridiculous it defies logic. It's like bashing a messenger that Hitler's coming, see that.

Living and working without people's confirmation is your greatest work undoing narcissism.

The way to your success is to lose respect for everyone else and their shallow pettiness.

CONTRADICTIONS AND SOUL TIES

The greatest of all lessons was how not to drink at contradiction which was all around.

Contradictions drive a genius biocomputer mad. Mixed signals, polite cruelties, the subtle crap.

Your soul tie with that poser/person blocked your work and dulled your vision. Get with it again.

To think you needed HIS approval. That's how sick you were before you knew, poor you.

He makes fun of you to his peanut gallery and you continue to take it honey? No way baby.

I once knew a brilliant genius female who needed the approval of a shallow narcissist she knew.

His sarcastic put-downs finally got to her and she came to herself, a creative magic elf.

LIBERAL LOSERS

She said "go to hell" to him and his minions, gofers, groupies, vapid admirers/dumb followers.

Hatred is subtle/between the lines but the brain reads contradiction: just get drunk tonight.

Jesus said: Who are your sisters? Those who love God--if liberal divide from those others.

When someone whose intelligence you respected turns out to be puerile I'd avoid it.

IT'S WHO YOU FOLLOW

If you hate Facebook or Twitter it's a reflection of who you follow or like. It reflects you, yikes!

For a woman to be with a narcissist like that she'd have to think what he thinks/confirm his crap.

Hatred is subtle/between the lines but the brain reads contradiction: just get drunk tonight.

Watch out when a man robotically says he loves you every two minutes—he's covering tracks.

For every SIN there's a compensation in the present moment and THAT'S how we know it.

How can you call Twitter/Facebook garbage, when it's purely who YOU follow that determines it?

BETRAYAL TRAUMA

A person IS what he IS and a dog returns to his vomit. Is he locked in the dark? Think about it.

Lord said be satisfied with wife's breasts for life but what of his seeing em on those sites?

LIBERAL LOSERS

Betrayal trauma is when the man you knew turns out to have the emotional maturity of two.

The nice lady said "he went thru my money like water, I gave the useless stuff to the neighbors."

She chose a weak man thinking he'd stay with her but as it turns out he just broke her heart.

She chose one with vulnerabilities thinking a good marriage more likely but he ruined her see.

Every single time she trusted again, forgave him again, just wanting peace and a happy homelife.

When "IT" happens again she's demolished again, devastated over and over and over and over.

PAIN IN THE SOLAR PLEXUS

The lady said "my gut feels like a horse kicked it". That's the solar plexus sensing distrust.

The Betrayal Trauma survivor never trusted again, seeing the duplicity in her spouse or friend.

The solar plexus in the gut regulates the environment vis-a-vis me and the ACHE was PANIC.

The concentration camp survivors said they'd never trust human nature again, it's all sin.

The Betrayal Trauma survivor never trusted again, seeing the duplicity in her spouse or friend.

It's because all men are sinners that we can't trust anyone. Trust no man and rely on Him.

WHAT PEOPLE ARE LIKE

LIBERAL LOSERS

Female genius lacks women friends since due to the Jezebel spirit with trouble they disappear.

The Holocaust survivors saw how ordinary "decent" people became foes, that's all they know.

Realizing universality of sin and relying on Him transfers the pain so cast your care friend.

The social female will listen to the old bitty putting down all novelty then she'll hate you see.

Don't blame hurt, humiliation and pain on him, only on you trusting him again, again, and again.

Being rejected brings a trancelike spirit trying to prove them wrong and the self worthy.

LIBERAL TYRANNY

Liberal tyranny in families is so constant and dauntless i can still hear people yelling at me.

I'm sorry but you're just too boring, slow and vacuous for me to listen to anymore your highness.

His boring milquetoast bearing they call "humility" and they just love how he says NOTHING.

As a teacher when they flew paper airplanes at me I lost all my audacity/was too young see.

"He" is a nonpersonal pronoun for ALL mankind but girl stopped me: "you must say he AND she."

All this crap is nothing but intellectual speed bump and the ruination and block to true genius.

Yes slavery/racism was real but Americans went to war to change all that and no one else did.

LIBERAL LOSERS

Slavery was all over the world then and the meanest slaveowners were black and Arab sir.

The Nazis were mean & white but all men are sinners and have two sides, it's evil not racist.

For genius to come out it must be safe to unfold. In this social climate it's hard to be bold.

Genuis is audacious or caves in and regresses. Such audacity with novelty is difficult presently.

You already ridiculed & mocked me to your peanut gallery so I refuse the gig, I tested you see.

I can no longer adapt to your mediocre thing cuz I got my OWN thing and it's far more inspiring.

When they pounce with this stuff it's hard to fight back. I caved in enough, that's a fact.

HOLLYWOOD: EVILS OF AMERICA

Hollywood movies are critiques of the evils of America. It's so racist/all about the narrative.

Narcissistic injury is a challenge to grandiosity but mortification to the crumbling false self.

It's not so much husband abuse but that he becomes painfully oversensitive to her moods.

As a false self of narcissist crumbles it's unable to maintain pretensions and can't defend itself.

When grandiosity is massively undermined everything falls apart--the end of the the narc.

When the narcissist identity as a fiction is confronted by hard reality it falls and withers away.

LIBERAL LOSERS

Don't let em in cuz they want everything. Like kids once they see it they desire it, grasping.

DEALING WITH CENSORSHIP

Their censorship of you is a poor reflection on them only--practice seeing that honey.

Get used to rejection, censorship, condemnation, being called rude--see it as good.

You must retrain responses to rejection now. Stop being a narcissist wanting their love.

The more truth the more rejection. Get used to it, expect it/if they approve question it.

Avoid useless disputes over stupid controversies which produce nothing but strife see.

NASTY RESPONSES TO NOVELTY

The uneducated youth respond to novelty with nastiness. Anything different, they attack.

And they're all uneducated, coming from the public schools. Practice ignoring these fools.

As the insults pour out you gotta be tough/let it flow right off your back. Practice/look up.

If you wanna make a mark you must face the flack and that's greatness--it is "highness".

Don't respond to lowminds cuz they're bitter too and you don't need that anymore, you're kind.

Schools only gave em a line to learn by rote not know how to think so we're unequally yoked.

LIBERAL LOSERS

When they insult, cut em loose right now. If it's worthy debate fine but you're a champ you know.

HOME IS HEAVEN

Living in a violent society filled with duplicity home is our only chance for joy and tranquility.

Home is all where you walk tall. So make it reflect your personality as separate from the fallen.

Once your home is heaven, don't let em in. Use extreme vetting cuz it's spirits son.

Feminists had a saying on t-shirts: "F**k housework" and that started this horrible curse.

The movie "Harriet Craig" [1949] made hands-on creation of a nice home look like neurosis.

IF THEY DON'T GET IT, TOUGH

Trying desperately to prove to gainsayers is the residual symptom from the spirit of rejection.

If they don't get it don't bend over backwards explaining it, always reacting to nuts!

You've been dumbed thru the school system so how COULD you know what I'm sayin'.

Dangerous soul ties can even be formed by words with sex connotations-- watch every word son.

There's a line & you must stay on THIS side of that line. How do you find it? Be decent/kind.

Never taught how to think only to hate so they react to novelty with nastiness, hard to take.

LIBERAL LOSERS

Whoever supplies illusions is their master, whoever destroys them is their victim. Le Bon

Pandemics of mind spread the fastest in a mass psychosis where the norm is madness.

The specific manner in which mass psychosis unfolds depends on history and young/old.

SHADOW PROJECTSION

God's not gonna bless you with a buncha jerks around or wanna bes coming without being announced.

Seems like a peaceful neighborhood but get involved with any one of em you go down a rabbit hole.

The truth about people is they'll project their meanest shadow onto you, a lowly scapegoat.

Instead of turning me into the gestapo they created social conditions turning my free life into hell.

The unrecognized part of their badness [shadow] they only see in you. Get strong or die young.

Don't get involved with any one of the socials for inside there is a haunted house/confusion caused.

It is not enough to serve your sentence, there's collateral damage [hate] you have to deal with sis.

People minimize sex sin. They do their ex a favor and it's disgusting. Carnal beasts, all of em.

SCAPEGOAT MECHANISMS

Giving up liberty to be taken care of: this is the exact same matrix I had with the narcissist.

LIBERAL LOSERS

When all civility is lost towards a person--he's been branded--it all pours out, ugly hatred.

It's something you went through but will never happen again. A one shot deal, forget it man.

People are now so vapid and cruel get involved with any one and you're up the creek/screwed.

The best game plan is to stay alone until you find a mate who both understands and loves you too.

God knows the outcome but His children still go thru the test, something none of us gets past.

God's wrath comes in natural disasters but also in suddenly being surrounded by strangers.

I spent half the time desperately lonely and the other half hating all invasion no matter how petty.

They show you the monster when they know they have you--to move in and burn your bridges too.

HE WANTS TOTAL CONTROL

He wanted total control with me isolated and unable to escape once he showed me his true self.

They get angry and won't let you go until you agree with them--reminding of the snowflakes some.

He was an obvious sadist but without self-awareness--didn't have the faintest. I escaped, blessed.

70 year old psychopath is a damaged child who needs the partner-fix to be totally controlled.

Thru hyper-control the psychopath creates the conditions he perceives he needs to grow.

LIBERAL LOSERS

I could see him making the effort/always coming back so I mistook his hyper-control for love in fact.

Immaturity: I could see it had nothing to do with love but his controlling me like he **OWNED** me.

Most psychopaths aren't in jail, they walk among us as normal but drive us crazy in our houses.

He could not allow a tranquil existence, it was impossible for him. He had to created chaos/bedlam.

It was frightening to be treated as an owned object. It was like I was subhuman or didn't exist.

He made me mentally weak by doubting all my decisions and everything I stood for down to the core.

NARCISSISTS ARE PSYCHOPATHS

The reason most narcissists are also psychopaths is due to their lack of conscience.

Explosive anger marks the narcissist and I can relate to that. I was apprehensive every minute.

His posture would rise up against me [threatening physically] controlling what I do or say.

TEMPER: He could change in a second and get really aggressive--my fear of him got depressive.

Sudden explosive anger then blame me for whatever. It was like living in a grenade range, I swear.

Always walking on egg shells: we'd be at the beach having a great time and suddenly it was hell.

He'd stop the car suddenly and say "what are you thinking about?" like I committed a felony.

LIBERAL LOSERS

If I was thinking about my own thing--preoccupied from him--he'd push me out to hitchhike home.

ALWAYS SEE THE SYSTEM

Suddenly I had to defend myself for something I didn't do. It was always something and he'd stew.

Psychopaths are damaged children blocked from normal development and thus very demanding.

With arrested development/no theory of mind they can't take into account others are a different kind.

The stuff I'm bringing thru is beautiful and deep now--not bringing thru lower archetypes anymore.

It wasn't "me" it was a demon plus immaturity, lack of knowledge/no self-confidence/being jealous.

It doesn't matter what they think, people on their way to hell--they made your life miserable you know.

I'm a psychologist who loves God & knows people. Not evangelist or preacher, for women are not to.

DO THEY HATE WOMEN?

The men seem to hate women and do mean things to them like leave em off to hitchhike home.

She's so freaked out with "love" chemicals from his meanness, template of the early trauma.

The men seem to have contempt for women, is this a new phenomenon? Perhaps its feminism.

He acted like he had a monopoly on the truth. The more I think about it I must be a narcissist too.

LIBERAL LOSERS

Whether it's about books, music or attitudes towards people, his opinion was the only truth.

I coulda been killed by those people but God saved me at the last minute every time cuz He hates evil.

The reason you have these horrible flashbacks is cuz you were hanging out with chumps and tramps.

You were such a weak twit to ever let em in but once you did you come complaining to friends?

This most important is to NOT let anyone in but you let everyone in so now have PTSD symptoms.

Prescription for mental health: [1] set boundaries and [2] build assertive power to maintain them.

Boundaries are the most important thing for man is hyper-suggestive in the contagion of madness.

Hyper-suggestive in the contagion of madness: that's social psychology, or the herd of asses.

SOCIAL CHARM

Social Charm: They were chumps and tramps with status so you saw them as the most your highness.

You're into success so stop flashing back to the preparatory stage, you're way past that.

When they came in I couldn't wait to get rid of em. It's too much at this point, mental bedlam.

To "toughen" you I show you what people are like. That's all you need to know, tell em to take a hike.

I was made to feel like I was over-sensitive until after the relationship then I could not believe it.

LIBERAL LOSERS

Most don't recognize narcissistic abuse due to lack of knowledge so getting this is most important.

Psychopaths try to convince the prey that she is crazy rather than being happy for me see.

When the psychopath succeeds in making her doubt herself he weakens her tremendously.

Doubt very quickly makes us loose our energy, self-confidence and all defenses [hedges].

The narcissist doesn't see reality he filters and reinterprets it to buttress his grandiosity.

He says "that never happened, I never said that" cuz it conflicts with his self-image of a cool cat.

Since everything is filtered thru him you can't test your truth so everything he says is the truth.

She cheated on him/he felt aggressive so she found him a therapist for that, not her deceptiveness.

HE TURNED EVERYTHING AROUND

He turned everything around. He said I was using him though he lived here like it was his home.

It's all reversed. If he says you're financially holding back you can be sure he's doing stuff like that.

It was when I was strong that he'd criticize, belittle me and keep me hostage for hours, screaming.

When I was down he'd switch like a button/be so sweet to me as a lady condemning all my enemies.

Homeostatic system: being up brings sting-shots and flip flops but being down brings pep-talks.

LIBERAL LOSERS

The same one trying to destroy you when strong is giving you comfort if weak and you soak it up.

Confusion and doubts: Oh he's nice to me now, maybe he's not such a bad person after all.

Since narcissists rely on you not relying on self they need to target that which they do with stealth.

For survival I was brainwashed, forced to ignore all the glaring red flags and unhealthy bad stuff.

He pushed me outa cars, he killed me pets. And yet I was supposed to never mention it and I didn't.

Tho' isolated he introduced me to one friend from whom I would soon rent. Secretly I arranged it.

The more you're unsure of your personal reality the more you are fresh meat for the predatory.

It got to where nothing existed without his permission. The loss of my reality was a sickening feeling.

When they tear down statues of Lincoln and Grant it's not re: civil rights but hating America.

I could hear people yelling at me and thought a fast would solve the problem and it did: inner silence.

LACK OF EMPATHY

Not only will he not stop when you beg him to he feels he's the right to abuse you and continue.

Narcissists never take responsibility—if you're hurting it's cuza something you did and that's it see.

They never assume guilt or blame, they are always the victimized party and they believe it ok.

LIBERAL LOSERS

In a land where everyone's traumatized, everyone's a narcissist cuz that's the self's defense.

When the narcissist comes across as the victim tho' the culprit he's not acting, he truly believes it.

PEOPLE ON THE PROPERTY

Anytime you let people on your property it opens the door to their stuff/friends/family without remedy.

Every time someone hooks up on the property they bring their friends, habits, thoughts, stuff, family.

You don't just get "them". You get all of their internal conflicts spilling out into chaos/bedlam.

Out of empathy/altruism he allowed them to hook up in our homestead and they totally ruined it.

Every dam time I took someone in they ruined me. They aren't like the grateful dogs and cats see.

You're not just taking a person in but perhaps a huge inescapable burden, I'm talking demons.

It's not that I swayed from the truth but after swimming in muddy waters I just got lukewarm.

BEING HATED

I recall what being hated feels like and when it's unwarranted like that it's a scapegoat device.

The woman woulda done anything to shut me up, ruin my rep, make me look illegit, a dumb twit or slut.

Lay down/enforce boundaries and the great reward is world renowned success cuz God can bless.

LIBERAL LOSERS

They were so jealous of me living way out in the country they were compelled to come/bother me.

Don't let em in cuz it's opening a door to possible demons and your home life will go downwards.

You spent years building a home up, why take a chance by letting in those who never chose it?

We all have stories to tell of the wild wild west living in the human jungle and it's also God's will.

Choice #1. Go with Satan and live a lavish lifestyle until he destroys you with God's authorization.

Choice #2. Build a better world or stay blissfully ignorant calling your good friends haters and bigots.

DISCARDING AND HOOVERING

When you think of him, think: poor character. Don't give him the time of day or again you're the loser.

Every cycle has a beginning and an end. This one is ENDED and now never go back my friend.

Don't envy when the petty flourish like a green tree for just as suddenly they're mowed down, trust me.

Somewhere along the way he decided I wasn't good enough and discarded me--it was tough.

The problem with bingeing to control shame is that binge eating actually perpetuates the cycle of shame.

Why would we want a rejector? That is the whole question/why we're not a whole person.

My core wounds were HEALED when I was finally seen, heard and understood. New life: connection.

LIBERAL LOSERS

With each day of no-contact you'll feel so much better not obsessed with this creep your rejector.

The narcissist always circles back--it's called the "hoover" so you get good at blocking: emotion-remover.

As you're growing he sucks you back into the dynamic but each time you resist you're stronger for it.

Why want a rejector who disappears when you can have great conversations with a true, loving peer?

You have an inner circle of totally trusted associates and everyone else is on probation 'til further notice.

You trusted far too easily/quickly, that was the embarrassing/immature trait in your history.

LET THE FANTASY DIE

Let the inner fantasy die, the false self they presented, the hormones and oxytocin creating the trauma bond.

He built the trauma bond thru intermittent reinforcement, blowing hot/cold, mixed signals, pulling back.

Why the hell be addicted to a person who is damaging you psychologically like this? Wake up sis.

There's no resolution with the narcissist who wants to keep you in a state of chaos vs. fantasy bliss.

When they go cold you want them to put their mask back on but they won't, it's over--go no-contact.

You must grieve the loss of the fantasy of who they pretended to be, NOW you can truly see.

They may act like they want you to succeed but guess what--they are lying, you must go no-contact.

LIBERAL LOSERS

Protect your inner child, peach/joy and debit card--most importantly, who you let into your house.

RECAP: Your life will be ten times better once rid of this person, this narcissistic hot-cold feller.

DIGNITY AND BOUNDARIES IS EVERYTHING

Nothing should be more important to you than your **DIGNITY** and your **BOUNDARIES. NOTHING.**

Porous boundaries began in childhood even by someone not recognizing your truth/being misunderstood.

Setting boundaries is a life of **CHOOSING** between self-respect or having fun as he pressures/expects.

She got so tired of the **FATIGUE** from constantly wanting him, the source of bitter and sad confusion.

Millions carry torches for rejectors--perhaps their whole life--not knowing poor character creates strife.

You're rare/have few people you can talk to and suddenly you meet him--your disappearing cuckoo.

This is hurt and pain you never have to feel again. Letting him go signals the angels to send the Real One.

Like the **FLOTUS** said: never give ear to a man who doesn't love **YOU** deeply, to you he's dead.

Cultural mores are constantly shifting around sex. Nowadays there is gross talk everywhere: sick.

IT'S STILL PERVERSE

To hear old men and women talking perverse is such a fall from dignity, their traditional right as elders.

LIBERAL LOSERS

You can't make someone have class. No matter what you do if with them you'll degrade and it's repetitious.

In any situation from any one, you must insist on total respect. NEVER give in for them, look up.

If not respected properly you must set a boundary and walk away--the number one rule each day.

The youtube guru who talks about sex incessantly to shit-shot his female fan base, watch for these.

BE READY TO SET BOUNDARIES/WALK AWAY

Any time be ready to set a boundary and walk away. "This doesn't feel respectful" you may be thinking.

If you go against self-respect by having a good time it'll always circle back to haunt you lest denying it.

As the bell-shaped curve accepts perversity you'll be pressured to accept it, see? Pass test, be free.

If they ghost you/don't return your text that is DISRESPECT. Simply ban him then on to the next.

Jenna: The vids you make so explain the fake I'm getting stronger each day after a life of being prey.

Above all stop fantasizing about him/her. This is part of the fake, energized by a trauma bond earlier.

If you don't shut down disrespectful conversation without setting a boundary you're a loser honey.

Setting good boundaries--a line in the sand--is also known as Good Ego Strength, being healthy.

The contagion of madness comes from porous boundaries and weak ego strength=giving in.

LIBERAL LOSERS

You want healthy relationships where you're equal: treated properly without pain/confusion [shoddily].

BUSTING BOUNDARIES IS FIRST

Even if it's a movie star busting your boundaries you must ALWAYS, always assert yourself immediately.

If a man talks too much about sex, get rid of him. This is a clear sign he's evil and you will be the victim.

Any talk of sex is between a man and his wife, not broadcast to the multitudes destroying lives.

HAVE FUN then be walked over and regret it. Putting self-respect first nips it in the bud and you're over it.

Letting losers walk over you that way brings more disrespect and it just gets worse I expect.

You self-defeat by enjoying their company while allowing tiny instances of disrespect to occur. Jenna Ryan

When we allow others to bulldoze over us tho' our heart feels disrespected, we may as well be dead.

Don't rock the boat--keep the fun going. NO: Take a stand and get the hell away from this gang.

FRENEMIES WHO SOW DISCORD

By smooth words/flattering speech they deceive the hearts of the simple. It's scary cuz they don't know you.

The enemy sows discord and division to simple minded people who can't discern truly good from evil.

You're not even supposed to reason with a fool, yet these simpletons are your enemy's army against you!

LIBERAL LOSERS

These are not my words, the bible says it--they deceive the hearts of the SIMPLE to agree with evil.

A simple person doesn't have discernment nor the mind of Christ. He doesn't think with logic and reasoning.

Solution to Frenemies: See them. Remember it was Joseph's brothers who sold him into slavery.

Never tell them your plans, aspirations or achievements--esp. your problems! Tell a perfect stranger, it'd be better.

Disengage slowly, walk away gently. The simple get mad but if it's gradual soon you're gone/the world fills in.

You must distance yourself from that negativity, jealousy and other unnerving tendencies in frenemies.

You don't have to be nasty to set a boundary. You don't have to be angry to call em out but do it today.

I know who I am, what I've accomplished and overcome. It took great strength and my bullies were bums.

You weren't validated for those things that make you who you are--the narcissist hates the star.

The narcissist is envious of your gifts, callings, talent, abilities. Those things ensuring your future, see?

THE NARCISSIST ENVIES YOU

The narcissist envies your warmth, your ability to speak in front of a crowd, how you light up a room: BOOM!

It's an evil experience being in the presence of envy. I can recall my sad childhood knowing my sisters hated me.

The bullying took it's toll in three decades of feeling like a clown with dangerous foes all around, the hedge down.

LIBERAL LOSERS

The more wimped out I became the more they saw me as inferior, worthless and inane. It was spiraling.

Fallen Hero Syndrome can happen to anyone--a biological process vis-a-vis the group since time begun.

An empath may not realize the other person is envious, he wants to believe the best so he can just relax.

As an embattled sad empath you can't see why they're envious--you're trained to look down on yourself.

To know their stance, check their interactions: do they downplay, devalue and dismiss your actions?

They were jealous of my gifts and callings. They called it "delusions of grandeur" they learned in psychology.

The best things about me they treated as a disease to be locked up--but my Father protected me nonstop.

Narcissists aren't going to celebrate your accomplishments and who you are. Remember that now, Star!

They're not gonna celebrate your graduate degree or cute facebook pic--to them it's all a lie or sick.

Or they may "celebrate" but you can TELL they're not truly happy for you. Block these frenemies or be blue.

If they're envious it's of EVERYTHING. How you get right back up after a downfall--your annoying resiliency.

They don't want you validated in your own success. They want to steal the spotlight or create a mess.

Go to dinner with a narcissist--they won't bring up your accomplishments, they'll deny you even exist.

YOU SHOULDN'T EVEN EXIST

LIBERAL LOSERS

Remember: to a narcissist you shouldn't even exist except as a mirror or pawn for what **THEY** have to offer.

She was even envious of my inner peace and sought to disrupt that any way she could without cease.

They feign an interest in you then devalue you to the others --you can always tell these hypocrite losers.

She would give me just enough attention and validation to trust her then imperceptibly smash me/my future.

After causing me so much trouble I rejected Jezebel on the double then she accused me of being hateful.

Tho' inwardly feeling inferior they have a superior complex and can't tolerate anyone on their level or higher.

If they get narcissistic supply from your accomplishment they'll piggyback on it but never validate you for it.

Learn to say: I'm so happy for you, I **KNOW** how hard you worked for this, the many hours--you deserve this sis!

They never brought it up at all--any accomplishment they denied or glossed over. I **NEVER** felt I was clever.

Envious people will never champion anything about you. They're "dead" set in the story of humans/shrews.

If abused narcissistically you become indifferent and unaware of your own accomplishments--amen?

I got so used to playing second fiddle I didn't notice when people devalued my accomplishments--just forget it.

When people aren't giving you credit where credit is due, your not noticing it shows the true travesty too.

SELF-ABANDONMENT IS STAYING QUIET

LIBERAL LOSERS

When you go along with this--peace at any price--it's like self-abandonment tho' unaware you're doing it.

If you go along with this you're in collusion with the others in the system to be ignored. Alan Robarge

Some envy-victims become overachievers driven to get those accolades. I can relate to that, in spades.

Dear Lord what I went through to get visibility in my family of origin when all they wanted was rid of me, envyin'

But as mom always said, it all evens out in the End. It made me strong/resilient in lucrative workaholism.

Attach yourself to a star, work yourself to the bones--just so someone will notice/applaud but then you're old!

We deserve to be around others who validate us/give credit where it's due--and to toxic enviers, pooh.

As you come out of the narcissist realm--the principality--you feel a right to be respected in true freedom.

The way she treated me. I'm less-than, my accomplishments didn't exist, I was depressed.

Women, think of all the girl friends you've known. Were you not victimized even if she's from a good home?

How did you adapt? My succumbing/conforming to exactly what they want THEN they would let up.

The message: No matter WHAT you've accomplished, your needs don't deserve to be met. ANGUISH.

KEY TO JOY: RECOGNIZE NARCISSIST SYSTEMS

Key to joy: recognize narcissistic systems who won't see who you are. Go no-contact if necessary/keep afar.

LIBERAL LOSERS

Close the door on those committed to ignoring you. Their worst fear is your fame and fortune--cruel.

Just find people who are happy for you so you don't have to jump their "hoops of fire"--now you'll feel better.

They'll downplay, downgrade, dismiss. devalue everything about you--except your eras of pain, their food.

When your remorse brings you pain: You're suppose to be abhorrent of your sins then God forgives em.

If you've accomplished much his ears perk up but to be narcissistic supply you must also be a doormat.

Get ready for the devaluation, get ready for the discard. Cuz you're a doormat and they're on top.

If you've got issues not worked through, then despite your accomplishments narcissists love to trigger you.

Broken childhoods wanna hope for validation from another person since they don't have validation within.

THE BROKEN LOVE NARISSISTS

A broken person will believe in the narcissist who ignores him while selling him expensive swampland.

I decided to be known for what I love or represented as opposed to what people thought of me esp. the bullies.

I stayed low/stored up strength until that moment I made my **BREAK** and exploded into destiny and fame.

I stayed low—putting up with you/you/you. I stored up strength: I didn't act, until now I used constraint.

Putting breaks on strength is Patience. Waiting/watching for miracles like a mouse watches a mousehole. Jung

LIBERAL LOSERS

I will not act/only react rightly to events as they occur, moving point by point without a plan just a prayer.

The over-regulated liberal state is always the same thing: punish achievers, reward bad behavior.

Obstruction in America: never-Trumpers, race hustlers, poverty pimps and the godless liberal media.

It may not be deliberate genocide but the effects are the same if white people are being totally replaced.

The Kalergi Plan of 100 years: make the world one mono-brown with the white people all gone.

BOUNDARIES AND LOST HEDGES OF PROTECTION

The cultural shift is seen in architecture of La Mesa or Borrego: houses on street without fences: social.

People banged on my door day and night. Now I'm behind walls and I can't BELIEVE the relief/got back my fight.

The elder lady preferred a rest home rather than stay home enduring her daughters friends hanging: this is WRONG.

A very sneaky, weird and sinful trend: billionaires becoming leftists with no concern for the poor.

European houses on the street without fences but with HUGE impenetrable door/atrium or home entries.

Must separate with clear divisions from outer world: atrium, garden, gate, guard rooms, living upstairs.

This isn't the fifties anymore, ok?. We must face that: tho' we love fifties movies that's just for nostalgia sake.

A billionaire accumulates wealth to escape society but when he gets it he must re-ingratiates himself to it?

LIBERAL LOSERS

TAKE A DEFENSIVE STANCE

Americans have been so socially hypnotized they let in everybody and for survival must be re-educated.

Just cuz you're super rich doesn't mean the super rich accept you cuz the pecking order's quite stratified.

The Old Money people are well educated and the new rich upstarts can't even talk so there's the first break.

Low intelligence [IQ] means also NO consideration for the animals so consider that when admitting immigrants.

I'm a Puritan, a complete prude and exquisite housekeeper like a hotel. A Calvinist, a Presbyterian I'm told.

I'm only happy as a good little girl. I hated those mean boys always invading me, they were dark, bizarre.

The guest of the billionaire is expected to entertain the host so a "guest" isn't easy, gotta be always up.

THIEVING GUESTS

The billionaire's guests take everything in the room. The communist spirit is everywhere, it's liberal.

We're talking about new money more than old money. It's a culture where visible wealth is important honey.

Mass illegal immigration leads to a lower quality of life, socialism, garbage/feces in the streets, distrust.

The destruction of the social fabric and the texture of life before mass immigration brings insanity, disease, loss.

Now they can look like smelly hillbillies and its all ok. Well some of us won't put up with it. Shave!

LIBERAL LOSERS

Don't ever accept a wrong as a right because the minute you accept it, it controls you with dark not light.

They're mean to everybody, not just you. It helps to see the universality of it now.

They don't get her, she's different. They talk to her sisters who hate her and suddenly they're all in.

I never see anyone cuz they're all in their households. Quiet, order, predictability, security, folksy.

You had to go thru all of it—trudging for decades—to get to here: pure. Thesis — antithesis, then dominate.

And it was **HORRIBLE** seeing the other side. Yuk three times! I feel sorry for myself now, but I survived.

DISORDERLY MESSERS

After coming from an orderly home it was sickening to see the effects of disorder and the kids were messers.

Due to the ACLU the thug brats rule in small towns and they know it. Don't ask me why, I can't explain it.

Grandma won't correct em since as a false Christian she forgives all things/says she didn't even see it.

You don't understand. Only the cross removes the **STING** of shame. That's the point, you're washed clean.

If someone complains her kids broke all of their windows, she denies all the glass on the floor.

After a period of struggle, rebirth.

One of the greatest delusions of salvation is a fixation on religious activity or "feeling spiritual"—it lulls.

LIBERAL LOSERS

Looking back at all the obstacles shows great danger but God took ya thru them all without realizing it sir.

If people are willing to turn on their neighbors and shoot em in a ditch they can certainly backstab/switch.

Cuz I didn't want to hangout they wanted to kill me. That's a social generation, taking it as an insult/blasphemy.

Fast for five days. Join the elite by not-doing. It's easy and quite a relief and deep rest from everyday living.

It was horrible living with a buncha liberals cuza their dirty minds. If you love dogs they'll say it's bestiality.

IT'S ALL PROJECTION

They have dirty minds and accuse others of what they are doing. It's always that way and it's been frustrating.

We the decent have been attacked from all sides. And it's been decades and continuing now as it increases.

They'll immediately call you friend and that brings obligations—miss em and they'll crack down.

You're not their friend/you're their slave.

A Dionysian generation is social also. The self-disciplined man is a loner and persecuted by the low.

I was shocked in kindergarten and more shocked thru all the grades and even college, esp. graduate school.

They were sickening and terrifying and I didn't want to go to school. Later on to adapt I just used alcohol.

Excuse me, you remind me of someone I used to know. Arrogant, a plagiarist and a dam fool know it all.

LIBERAL LOSERS

What gives you the right to "decide" about the subtlety of MY work? What makes you so superior jerk

I call it **SUBTLE** cuz it's a style I've been given and only I can describe it, like Johannesse Verse twit.

Build it, they will come. God will draw em to it and it'll be massive/a large sum.

Just cuz I forgave you'all doesn't mean I won't write about you or use you as an example of raging wolves.

What is a real man? He pays the bills and protects me/our home and that's the bottom line for millennium.

A home is not just walls but an amalgamation of personalities, their DNA, it is everything to me.

They say "we don't want revolution" so they can plausibly deny before they trigger it.

IT'S ALWAYS OP-TRUTH

It's always OP-TRUTH: They DO wanna civil war but blame it on us. They're getting ready to false flag/trigger it.

If you invert what they say, nine times outa ten you'll get the right answer. Alex Jones

They agree to look reasonable for few months hoping you don't have a memory then they trigger false flags.

Most people aren't like a Karen Kellock who gets more hardcore under attack—most just sell out.

It's best not to know rather than to know and still do it. Jesse Lee Peterson

ALONE IS BRIGHT, A CROWD'S A BLIGHT

God make a show of how much you love me so bullies who hate me will stand there slack jawed. Psa 86: 17.

LIBERAL LOSERS

So happy alone but with you it was a big black cloud that made me sick—feeling dark, unloved, kidnapped.

Having you come around was so horrible. It changed my joy to darkness/fear, I became emotionally unstable.

Being the sensitive one I became the identified patient but I was a victim of you—it all started with you.

You did the same thing—pulled the same frame up—with your husband and mother. Feminism is a killer.

Women make the darkest bullies. It's truly sickening with them in control, who's worse? I don't know.

JEZEBEL SPIRIT AND CRYING JAGS

The Jezebel Spirit causes crying jags. I think it's due to the unfairness under her tyranny and frame-ups.

She's so filled with demons from all her connections any involvement leads to spells of feeling maudlin.

It's not so much her as it is the army she brings in against you and you can sure tell she's been gossiping too.

Those are her sidekicks she primes thru sex and it's the oldest trick in the book of female bullies, like a hex.

God forgave me for being an arrogant bully but life taught me real fast thru human tragedies and raw reality.

A sickening arrogant feminist coming around casting doubts on MY reality since it wasn't HERS: creepy.

Acting so dam uppity and superior since the culture confirms her esp. the women's shows, corny.

Their smugness comes from the "obvious" cosmology we-are-one which is a falsehood leading to INSANITY.

LIBERAL LOSERS

More and more evidence is mounting that our president did nothing: the dems are underwhelming/boring.

THE POINT OF RELIGION IS RELATIONSHIP

The point of religion is a personal relationship with God. To do that we follow scriptures and know the word.

Impulse trumps intellect until you're sick of it—making mistakes due to sin when you mis-intuited it.

Being unprotected was the worst possible prison. Being protected is the most possible blessed freedom.

Who said I was your friend? I choose my own friends and friendship with you is too high maintenance.

You say we're friends and the next thing I know you'll be borrowing something or coming without calling.

You've reached the point of fame when everyone's on probation cuz you're so sick of the impositions.

So you can't trust anyone at the top—but you couldn't trust anyone on the bottom, at least now you're protected.

Being unprotected on the lower end—without a hedge or a fence—taught me more than a library of books.

MASTERING FEAR AND LONELINESS

I had to learn how to not get killed. Young men are taking over small towns and cops allow it all: ACLU.

In order to escape a small town gang I had to master fear of being alone on 1000 acres, the ghost town.

But then when they came around occasionally, I also had no protection and thus began my Ph.D. in the Streets.

LIBERAL LOSERS

Now I can imagine what the poor parents of these ruffians and Jezebels went thru: high school grads of 1985.

I wonder what they're like, in their fifties now. What happens to crazy kids as they age? Tell me, ok?

LET EM IN: LETHAL DANGER

As my PTSD diminishes I can clearly see the lethal danger I was in living alone in the desert, we see things later...

I would never do that today, the Obama years took my naiveté away. There's evil on all sides, pray.

The kids want what they want without the maturity to delay gratification nor the moral structure to say no, so...

Here's a free lesson in the natural sciences: Men don't have periods/vaginas nor women penises.

Bible is antithetical: in opposites. You let em in cuz you had no confidence/now you don't cuz you're fixed.

INTERLOPERS AND IMPOSERS

Your interlopers/imposers were your best teachers about ugly human nature. You had to learn it to mature!

Ugly human nature WANTS YOUR STUFF. You can feel a pull from em, even as a Jezebel wants your husband.

Jezebel wants your husband just to show you up. It's all about balancing forces, getting back, staying on top.

Jezebel wants your stuff whether she needs it or not. It's a sucking spirit and it's based on your total replacement.

The Jezebel spirit in the churches is quite frightening. They're so sure they're right condoning sinning.

LIBERAL LOSERS

As a Christian you are not condemned but THEY are due to their calumny—wrecking your reputation, ok?

SAINT COUPLES

Living separately on a plot of land is the greatest luxury. I have protection, solitude and see ya whenever honey.

Saint couples protect each other's solitude and that is the highest high there is and very powerful too.

The worst mate is one who has lax, lazy boundaries and lets people in on you as if social is expected too.

You protect my solitude: You protect me from the mean greedy world and if you don't I'm a very sad girl.

And I will protect you from the world always drawing you away into its cobweb of trivia and immorality, ok?

And once you have TWO protected solitudes you have the clarity/power of God UNOBSTRUCTED, full throttle.

But the false church is constant obstruction to genius solitude. It tracks into social and boring turpitude.

I'm not social I find it boring as hell and my God NEVER said it was the way to salvation, a lie He dispelled.

He NEVER said I was to be social at church, chatter with the ladies go to potlucks to be saved in the books.

I'm totally introverted in the amazing INNER journey and anything that distracts from that irritates: fact.

After the inner journey I have with my Lord how could I adapt to a false church? I'd be bored, besmirched.

The false church is most of em. It's rare you find one who goes by the literal word or puts down that horrible sin.

LIBERAL LOSERS

ABHORRENCE OF OUR SIN BRINGS FREEDOM

It's good to feel remorse since it's our ABHORRENCE of our past sins that leads God to totally remove em. Mark

Intelligence will only take you so far and good luck always runs out. Thelma and Louise

I had to go thru all that—you were my Ph.D. in the streets. Just letting you in reflected my dumbness/naiveté.

Music opens up so many more doors in the mind, if only they could see: the videos track it into empty.

If you truly abhor past sins then you're a changed person since before you had a seared conscience about em.

FRUITFUL REVERIES

Not always doing something. By far the most fruitful is just looking out the window, musing with pad and pencil.

This is why Soren had on his gravestone: "Now I'll be in valleys sweet, just with Jesus will I speak."

I'll be leaving but what I've given you is a social science matrix: the influence of human relationships.

You can be so happy alone then when another enters he ruins your game, destroys your reality, brings ill fame.

I felt compelled to let them in my home. I didn't see it as sacred but vulnerable when spirits enter or I was alone.

Even after they brought me down I continued to let them in when they came around—wow, I've come so far God.

Mom left me without defenses against the world—I was just told to be nice and be a good little hostess.

LIBERAL LOSERS

The more educated you are in America the more terrified you are to express what you think. Jared Taylor

Consistency is discarded while complexity, nuance, depth and profundity are replaced by simple threats, force.

WORKING THRU TRAUMA IS A PROCESS WITH AN END

Align yourself with stable people, visionaries who have goals and a to-do list, and avoid lazy losers.

Founders: Principals only work if there is integrity in marriage, industriousness, religiosity, honesty.

I'm taking it slow. I'm not gonna rush into a quick-fix then have to pull back and grow. You take over now.

You look like someone I always knew. Way back in consciousness, it's uncanny really--a relief too.

f you are quirky, don't try to be cool cuz people will love you for your quirkiness--embrace it. George Bruno

70% of women say their EX was abusive--she tells your family, friends, support groups and won't stop it.

When they get married she's a woman of quality but whon they divorce she's a heinous bitch out to get me.

People will always influence you so pick wisely. Mexican Playboy

My idea of winning was achievement and success, his was longshot windfalls he waited for in a rest.

Write your own script: Don't put procrastinators, messers, junkards, losers, couch potatoes and porn addicts in it.

Kill off those characters. Don't put em in the next script. George Bruno

Women were taught by mothers how to be a good wife and treat a husband---but now they just keep bitchin'

LIBERAL LOSERS

WRITE THE TRUTH NOT WHAT "SELLS"

You can't write for money. That's writing what they like rather than the truth--are you kidding me?

Write the truth then pray some day they'll read it--perhaps after your death, but even then it's all worth it.

A writer writes, a painter paints. The minute you think of SALES you've lost that natural talent and it stinks.

How is talent lost? ANOSIGNASIA--flipping into the left brain. Can't see patterns, you're just not great.

Through the right-brain man sees patterns, but thru the addictive left he can't--and fails like a blind bat.

Come off like a brilliant creative scholar or like a dam fool and a joker--all dependent on [L-R] where you are.

From the creative right to the hard left is a total change of personality, selections, performance--what a dunce.

Just saying the truth as I see it, which is all anyone can do.

When the bible says "trust no man" it ain't no joke. You can get your heart broken if unequally yoked.

It's all gonna be mental telepathy now. I'm done writing and speaking, gonna let the nonverbal kill the foe.

I hate the other way of writing--gives em a chance to run off at the mouth. Be PITHY: Just state the truth.

All preparations done/lessons learned, now it'll just happen. Relax, sit tight, get high, look at the sky.

BRACE FOR CULTURAL DECLINE

I've worked all my life for this moment. It's about to occur cuz it's pre-planned by God who always rewards us.

LIBERAL LOSERS

The contradictory fortune cookies say "beware of strangers"/"anticipate new people in your life".

Parents, you gotta watch your children. But you can't cuz you're wicked too-- the selfish motives of men.

They spoil their children from a hidden agenda of them covering up being wrong. Jesse Lee Peterson

Nothing could be more obvious that the genders, races and cultures are different but not to the ignorant.

I don't care if I don't talk to my sister/brother for the rest of my life, I'm not gonna agree that wrong is right.

You can't take em with you when you die, so what do all these commitments mean? Just to be seen?

How do you melt together with people you have nothing in common with--in a pot?

If you can't assimilate people into your society then your society collapses cuz you don't have one, see?

Pamela Harris platform died on the false mantle of diversity because the benefits of diversity are a MYTH.

Our "horrible patriarchy" is all about freedom, liberty, free speech, self-defense and the right to one's destiny.

All conventions are thrown to the wind by the left: an undisciplined, control freak grasping mob.

Real feminism is: girls do the work they want, not men coming into their bath room showing their ding dong.

ACADEMIC CREDITS FOR MORAL VIRTUE

But you don't get academic credits unless you spout "moral virtue" which is defined by them for you.

LIBERAL LOSERS

The lucrative diversity bureaucracy encourages protests which ends up extending their powers.

When Plato said "know thyself" he didn't mean to get into your many varied gender identities.

The dominant narrative is America's engrained sexism and racism and it's falsehood, it's evil vs. good.

Conservatives have one love affair after another with black politicians--so how could they be racist?

I've heard mushrooms are a poison, mushrooms are a superfood. Which is it? On pizza they're good.

MERITOCRACY: Race and gender are utterly irrelevant qualifications for a job short of fathering/mothering.

Young or old happens to everybody. Wherever you're at, you're on your way. Joyce Meyer

I'm trying to build an empire yet must deal with these petty things. Please don't make things worse, underlings.

NOT YOUNG AGAIN

I don't wanna be young again cuz I guess I *had* to go thru all that, a hell on earth which was so humiliating.

Mom never taught me those things, she didn't equip me. I had to go thru hell to learn it deep inside and keep it.

I completed my five day fast and the betrayal trauma. I'm ready to make him understand the depth of it all.

We must trust those closest or life is a rat's nest. A little distance is good once in awhile the bible says.

To learn all these lessons written here? It was hell--my Ph.D. in the streets-- dealing with women, men, fear.

LIBERAL LOSERS

What they put me through! But that's what happens if you're weak/in sin--you attract the same to you.

Now that we're purified by the blood we can rest assured things will change. For one thing, we have a hedge.

The consequences of sin are terrible--mostly because the punishments come from those around you.

And sinners are too **WEAK** to deal with these local obstructions to their destiny, so they fall quickly.

Elders, stop competing with youth! You think I could've built this empire if I were age 15? It took a lifetime.

Pornography in a marriage throws older achieved females in competition with youthful flesh--just think of that.

I'd like to be young knowing what I know now, but it doesn't work that way since I didn't grow up grounded.

WOMEN BLOCK FEMALE SUCCESS

She told me men were pigs and never to get involved with one. But what about the world and WOMEN?

Women and the female community were pure obstruction to me and female genius everywhere, it is **TYRANNY.**

They're friggin' mean witches if you don't think like them. I don't know where these officious harridans came from.

The betrayed wife can be so happy, then she's suddenly triggered and goes into a rush, slump or tragedy.

They treat age as if it's a disease. Not traditional respect maintaining the tribe as in the old days.

Unequally yoked: Pray for your enemies but you don't have to stay with them.

HOW CAN YOU WALK TOGETHER

LIBERAL LOSERS

Can two walk together unless they be agreed? Amos 3: 3

If your friend envies you you can't walk in agreement: unequally yoked, out of alignment.

A sound heart is the life of the flesh but envy is rotten to the bones. Prov. 14: 30

An envious friend is a dangerous enemy so treat them accordingly. This is no small thing, start vetting.

The Woke Culture is commensurate with the death of God and it's the religion of one with fake compassion.

Blue state mayors are focused on gender identity, climate change and unconscious bias not what's best for us.

I hide from BDD from low validation from significant others. Now I see I gotta get it from myself, God or whatever.

Before I love you, I'm gonna leave you. Takeaway Lyrics

Like a master of self-defense we have lethal power but don't use it--we're not bullies, just bully-proof.

It's the Art of Fighting without fighting. Bruce Lee

THE WEST IS THE SEAT OF LIBERTY

White people love to feel good about themselves by feeling bad about being white. Jared Taylor

The only thing left for weasel liberals: to look down on other whites as racist—this is their major thrill.

They do opposition research, try to figure out what makes Christians reject someone, then ruin him.

Poets are the unacknowledged legislators of the world. Percy Shelly 1821

LIBERAL LOSERS

Western civilization is seat of liberty, freedom and extraordinary accomplishment but we won't hear that.

Germany needs to develop a new approach dealing with aggressive men shaped by patriarchal cultures.

How fragile is a system where government is restrained by rules. All over the world tyranny is so cruel.

My identity's unimportant—it's what I know, what I've accomplished, what my beliefs are. Heather MacDonald

Unbelievably, parents of college students care more about prestige institutions than the actual education.

FROM CALIFORNIA CHAOS TO DECENCY

Dependence on mass immigration is a sign of societal weakness and a structural defect. Mark Steyn

From California chaos to order, decency, familial atmosphere, kids that obey, quiet homers.

What a difference an orderly society makes after being in that leftist atmosphere where kids rule us folks.

I've never been so creative since coming to middle America in a country neighborhood. Daily I start before midnight.

Trump said he wanted to give amnesty to the Dreamers—how many times must we win this fight? Ann Coulter

With the terrorists, we have to win every time but they win just one time and the country is over. George Bush

Jared Taylor is my hero cuz illegal immigration and the Great White Replacement is ALL he talks about.

Diversity comes side by side with a knife. You can't have one without the other, a form of white genocide.

LIBERAL LOSERS

Atomize a people, weaken their in-group preference.

Cultural relativism: the quixotic, progressive and utopian fantasy that all cultures are equal.

They get urges to vacation in dangerous countries so they can come back and virtue-signal to all their friends.

MARXIST PROFESSORS AND FEMINIST HATERS

When I think of how I let liberals bully me for decades. They were arrogant in those years and I cringed.

Arrogant professors thinking they knew better--having sex in their offices, the intelligent progressive sinners.

It was the sexual revolution and the faculty were the head of it--totally disgusting when you think of it.

Feminists crippling my ability to lecture since they'd stand up saying "you didn't say him AND her".

They had a saloon on campus and I made use of it. I hated being in this liberal atmosphere and felt desperate.

At first I found you conservative but soon the other creeped in. You're a liberal friend, you condone sin.

JOHN THE BAPTIST WAS A SIN HATER

What made John the Baptist so singular? He attacked SIN while most are like today, casually condoning it.

I attack sin cuz I was a sinner and it had such a grip on me--my life so unfree/a tragedy--but now I'm Me.

Sin will grip you and not let you go until you spiral down to hell--hitting bottom. So don't start, that's my motto.

The sin that brings the most poverty as a consequence is SEX SIN--some are rich but most are on the bottom.

LIBERAL LOSERS

God doesn't want you fooling around. We're to have a spouse for that is the basis of our civilization.

That's called **ATTACHMENT** for bio-survival. When that bond is broken the result is distress/betrayal trauma.

It took a lifetime to find out that faith in God, personal confidence and strength was the true Safe Space.

If raised in a narcissistic environment you won't be validated for those things they're envious of.

I see what I want and am willing to wait and pray for it. If God wants it it's mine but will never again chase it.

Men should be equally threatened by women getting together, they discuss you and they get dirty.

SOCIAL HYPNOTISM IN SYSTEMS

Women threatened by men getting together: there's usually a debasement, isn't there? No mystery

One disagrees with your truth and the whole gang comes against you. This siding against one is totally liberal.

When you feel this happening--scapegoatism, siding against one--escape the scene, block, unsub.

Father absence is incredibly toxic for most children. The results are catastrophic--the facts indisputable.

Female rulers initiate war **FAR** more than male rulers--a very important fact few people mull over.

With men taken out of the equation women marry government/socialism and we're all dead ma'am.

Of all the people you know, most are little demons here to hold you back. Vet everyone for safety/see it like that.

LIBERAL LOSERS

It's all about am I offended, rather than whether or not what you said was offensive. Ben Shapiro

It's not that our Hollywood friends are ignorant, it's that they know so much that isn't so. Mr. Reagan

UNBRIDLED HEDONISM

Unbridled hedonism in the guise of freedom, malignant self-worship in the guise of liberty. Days of Noah

Overcome the neurotic adults through fasting. Some teens have learned this secret which is creative-making.

They weren't "people" but demon actors and reprisals for your sins, repent and they are gone.

I decided to stop worrying about the books completely and just get rich. That answers all problems I confess.

The way you get rich is a lot of irons on the fire then kicking back cuz you've learned stress is danger.

If you're rich you're not thinking of **ANY** of these people but as a poor guy you're always thinking of em...hmmmm

Think rich **BEFORE** you're rich. Never take the victim role again or think of past persecutors or that witch.

Take control where you're not intimidated by these same people ever again. Think **ABOVE** the herd, man.

Take the **ETERNAL** view--that's your destiny. Fly above the herd like a bird, looking down on the whole tragedy.

Think: If you were filthy rich would you be worrying about the same people as you are now? This shows all.

CULTURAL MASOCHISM

LIBERAL LOSERS

Obsessive tattooing is called "cultural masochism"--isn't that interesting, I knew it was real nihilism.

It's as if people don't know they are real until the others signify their existence with a "like".

It all starts with a lack of God worldview followed by a severe trauma in childhood--was that you too?

These wayward children grow up with a huge void which is filled with a false self based on behavioral narcissism.

In a world where people refuse to take action the man who does take action is king. Owen Shroyer did it, see?

This inner void exaggerates the need for attention and recognition then fame becomes toxic narcissism.

The modern digital world is like staring into a mirror while completely ignoring everyone as if inferior.

Their clueless followers cannot differentiate between healthy and unhealthy, good/bad, moral/immoral.

In the sick and diseased culture, postmodern screens and memes has replaced truth and order it seems.

You do everything you can to set yourself up for success--the universe grants you a moment and you take it.

You take the side of wrong just because it's your relative. That's called nepotism and it's really bad.

FLUSH EM OUT

It isn't being Christian to suckup to a bunch of juvenile delinquents--that's being a doormat masochist.

Rather than warring on the enemy it's much easier to give em enough rope to hang themselves, you see?

LIBERAL LOSERS

Flush em out--draw out who he really is. Show how he isn't your friend and then it's the mark he misses.

This works for me. All I gotta do is live a good life and wait. They chose this route and I'm ready/out the gate.

They will war against you as God's own but God is your Champion--that's one of His attributes man.

Be NICE while you flush em out. SMILE while you rid the block. This is higher wisdom than your foe, a nut.

NEPOTISM AND AGREEING WITH WRONG

NEPOTISTS: Agreeing with wrong because it's a relative.

I long to live in a neighborhood where I'm not being victimized. We didn't pick any of this.

These are KIDS. Kids are the ones doing mean things like this. Adults wouldn't expend the energy/think of it.

KIDS: But because he's your relative you turn your back on truth--what he DID--and tell me to forget it.

A mother will go along with his deception to save her son--they cut corners for nepotism more than anyone.

The nice Christian Grandma forgave everything and always saw the best in him and then he went to prison.

Why do we now have women lecturing in the nude? Because it's the END of civilization dude.

I didn't want her Jezebel Spirit in my house. It was grasping, enveloping, imposing, untrustworthy.

As with Los Angeles and San Francisco, their utopian dreams led em right into destruction.

LIBERAL LOSERS

Preachy, agenda-driven and condescending: that's Hollywood movies and to us they're boring.

I'm very well seasoned after being smack-downed for many reasons--who'd wanna be young again?

I needed to lose everything and get really hurt by jerks to become my best so why feel remorse? Just rest.

Success is like a Tsunami--the tide dwindles to nothing then comes back 1000 x more, exploding.

FEMINISTS ARE NO FRIENDS

Be cautious of your feminist friends who will always advise you to sin. Dangerous allies--frenemies not friends.

If success is a Tsuinami starting with nothing and most suicides happen then, learn from that and get going.

Your feminist friends love to see you down or dirty. They'll misadvise you to sin heavily, they're demons really.

It was not 'til I got a moral compass/looked back with new eyes that I realized feminist friends were my enemies.

They will misadvise you to sin WHILE never giving credit when it is due. This is not a friend but a shrew.

The housekeeper was so jealous of her as the owner she robbed her blind and then gossiped about her.

Betrayal trauma triggers primal panic then the poor wife is the lunatic tho' innocent.

Betrayal trauma is biology not psychology. Animals connect--when there's a break it causes distress.

Esp. for the female who needs to feel safe and protected, this is a break in safety--she's dead/home is wrecked.

LIBERAL LOSERS

It's terrifying cuz it's biology at its most primal: early attachments and patterns suddenly broken.

When trust is a repair of the earlier trauma [deeper strata] then the new betrayal is lethal I'll betcha.

There's a leak--a generalization--as all prior events melt together in one big treacherous double standard.

It was not 'til I got a moral compass/looked back with new eyes that I realized feminist friends were my enemies.

I know I can't change anything but I can do my part. The world is going to hell and everyone's falling apart.

COMPLACENCY AND AGING

We heal, we get complacent, he gets bored and clicks on the wrong thing, it all lines up on the left, he's sunk.

They see aging as a wearing out of parts rather than a completion of greater wholes/seasoned in the arts.

The computer is the devil's tool to lure men in by the millions and few are strong enough to refuse it.

Middle aged wives competing with 15 year old porn queens get plastic surgery. What a tragic comedy.

It's amazing how sin takes you down a rabbit hole. Without control it escalates and you're no longer whole.

Even if I felt that it wouldn't be proper of me to say it so forget it.

Saints in monasteries existed on bread from their bakery, butter from their dairy and fun from the winery.

Hurt me on the deepest level. I can still recall the feelings in the gut. Now I just try not to think about it.

LIBERAL LOSERS

Self-comforting: just like any other addiction. Why do they call these things a disease--all sin works this way.

Its strange but I don't feel revenge, just sickening shock. It's strange cuz this time I didn't fight back.

DEPENDENCE-INDEPENDENCE CYCLES

I never understood his militarism but that's the difference between women and men--we need em/protection.

One bad habit multiplied a million times cuz you didn't nip it in the bud and now it shows in your reflection.

I thought he was God. But then I woke up and didn't take the bait--i feel so much better today.

He told me what I needed to hear to resolve my fears/dry my tears--narcissists are so good at that my dear.

He was able to brilliantly reflect back my deepest values, bringing me SO high so he could pop my balloon.

The brief journey into another's mind taught me more than a library of books cuz it was me who took the hook.

This is maturity: going through things like that and getting hurt, overcoming it then coming back strong and smart.

A narcissist knows how to get close to you psychologically so you can't help but love em already.

TEST OF LIFE

Test of life: refusing and eliminating what you're attracted to after finding out it's rot, and you're really not.

As a youth I went with my attractions which ended it destruction but now I choose logic and elation.

LIBERAL LOSERS

No matter how great and marvelous he seems if it's not part of God's scheme it's not the A-Team.

When I pulled back I thought I'd be blue but instead I was so happy and relieved because I overcame you.

Why so much on narcissism suddenly? It's about aging babies--an entire generation like you don't wanna be.

Narcissists seek their supply--YOU--and know just what to do, young boys learned it in the locker rooms.

But people aren't treating you this way anymore cuz now you're mature. This is PTSD making you remember.

You kept knocking my door, calling me rude cuz I wouldn't let you in rather than seeing you're the rude one.

SOCIAL HYPNOTISM AND REJECTION

It's been an ALL-SOCIAL generation since WWII so they were instantly shocked when they met a recluse.

The social thing seems convivial but it automatically bans the clear/creative who won't agree with y'all.

It's a matter of interactional synchrony and neurophysiology: they just hate you the anomaly.

They just hate you and don't know why. They can't put their finger on it but will slander until you die.

Interactional synchrony is a microscopic dance based on similitude but if different they "see" you as rude.

I must do my own thing and not adapt to you. Sorry but that includes ignoring the magnetism you exude.

You brag about how much sex you've had like it's a feather in your cap but I see you as a dirty ol' chap.

LIBERAL LOSERS

Those closest turning against me and him using it against me: these are the sick systems surrounding thee.

To recover from betrayal trauma ARM yourself against caregivers who will blame you for it Momma!

I remember the years of feeling hit from all sides, with none to help! I felt so desperate as I daily cried.

Being betrayed is a [BIOLOGICAL] break in safety, a Type One Trauma like in war or a bombed out city.

PTSD shows in thinking people are against you now when they aren't. Memory is triggered, seeming current.

Hate is not fear of their "differences". They're meanness to animals offends all sensibilities of us sensitives.

QUESTION YOUR ATTRACTIONS!

Mortification: The false self crumbles and the borders are down as evil invades/is allowed.

Duplicity is hard to deal with Sue. Robotically he says "I love you" but he looks at boobs too.

You see, I don't need you. I know God has a plan and I'm waiting for that man.

They call themselves "social" but you should hear how they talk about the odd girl staying away from it all.

I've been taught to thoroughly question my automatic attractions cuz I've been DEAD wrong before man.

Like a moth to the flame there I go again but this time I'm gonna constrain my natural tendency to be vain.

Heck no, God has a plan and I'll wait for that man and NOT get hung up with your map or where I don't belong.

LIBERAL LOSERS

Question your attractions cuz they're not logical just emotional probably from a prior strata or level.

Few can commiserate with the pain we feel. They have no way of relating to it--as if we're on an island all alone.

No matter how great and marvelous he seems if it's not part of God's plan it's not gonna be the A-Team.

Now I understand it's not a matter of a man--whether or not we lose him--for we've something higher than.

Thank God I'm able to put feelings on hold/search out the deeper issues of emotions using reason to withhold.

God's Plan is redeemable when we've repented and are again peculiarly adorable in His eyes, a marvel.

LIBERAL CREEP AND GLOBALISM

Everything they did is now our fault. We live in a universe that is contradictory, mixed up and arrogant with gall.

The Red-Green Alliance: The totalitarians of Islam bonded with the totalitarians of the left all around.

They want us atomized, not in groups. That's why ALL of this is happening if you see the whole scoop.

A scattered and individualistic population is easy to conquer, a force to be reckoned with no longer.

COLLABORATORS

The people who lower the drawbridge into authoritarianism are always the first ones to go into the meat grinder.

There are two reasons for mass shootings in every case: mental illness or Jihadists.

LIBERAL LOSERS

A maudlin hysteria has taken over college campuses today. Heather MacDonald

Because professor told em to choose their own Halloween costume, he got a 3-hour tirade after school.

There's a lucrative bond between self-engrossed students and the diversity bureaucracy that grows constantly.

You see the simplemindedness in ignorant students feeling entitled to berate and humiliate adults.

Feminist orthodoxy ruling Google: lack of gender parity in engineers indicates sexism and implicit bias.

Preposterously irrelevant criteria now governs the hiring practices in the sciences/humanities in colleges.

Don't give me advice: There are different predilections for competition and risk between males and females.

If females aren't proportionately represented it's by definition a result of sexism, despite lowered critoria.

DIVERSOCRACY MADNESS

There is widespread discrimination in women's favor in all departments, lowering the hiring criteria.

China is ruthlessly meritocratic and that's why they'll be getting speedily way ahead.

Like a sick insidious cancer spreads the Diversocracy. It is sickening to me as it is to you as we descend.

They act like they're living thru an epidemic of campus rape. They are not, males avoid the whole lot.

They use wild exaggeration/cherry picking saying "it's all awful" to a crowd of simpletons seeking downfall.

LIBERAL LOSERS

Of course they're simpletons—they can hardly read or write. They are graduated anyway so it looks right.

Now they're not accepting white male Ph.D. students since they won't get a job, lowering their placement stats.

The humanities are at the core of my being. That is why I'm so angry as it's replaced with a lower scene.

All that incredibly good European literature was replaced in the eighties with a scourge of identity politics.

It doesn't take a majority of people to subscribe to an ideology without it having an affect on our society.

The democratic party has been captured by identity politics. We go into a dark age not a Renaissance.

Tho' there could be another Renaissance of the greatest thinkers, I see us going into an eclipse phase.

"The enlightenment is the basis of racism"--what? The west changed everything like sadistic tribalism.

HOW STABLE MIDDLE AMERICA WAS

How stable life is in country middle America. But as Californian ex-pats flow in, it's the end of ya.

California ex-pats bring their dam gun control and their sex ed for kids protocol and we're SICK of y'all.

California ex-pats made rich from selling buy middle America, locals out-priced as state goes blue.

Why we love Trump: I' stuff done, not taking any bullcrap from anyone, making America great again.

Advice to women dating: Forget dating and just create your own home. Get into it totally, never to roam.

LIBERAL LOSERS

Clean and order every drawer, create mystery in every cranny. Build it, he will appear immediately.

Inside I hear people yelling at me. That's a psychological introject from another world, era and reality.

It may not be deliberate genocide but the effects are the same if white people are being totally replaced.

I speak the truth as I see it and am not responsible for what someone does who happens to agree with what I said.

THEIR OWN PEOPLE

All healthy people want the survival of their OWN people and that is a subject which is unimpeachable.

No-kill shelters are cruel. They sit in cages for life in order to be true to their clientele—this is dog/cat HELL.

Never settle the pet issue after you're married, only way before--don't let that start a war.

Hip hop was globalist inspired to drag the blacks down. Previous to '64 the father was in the home.

As whites timidly give them what they want it only gets worse for them as it sets them off.

My general philosophy is "live and let live" must mostly "get out of my face". Mark Levin

Marxism is a constant revolution, conservatism is a stand in place being hit all around.

Americans never decided our children should be taught that our country is inherently evil.

The 1619 Project rewrites our history with whites as villains & slavery made the system run.

LIBERAL LOSERS

Our founding fathers were incredible geniuses and of course they were flawed/all are fallen.

The border's down, they're flowing in by millions. The Northwest is burning, we must hide son.

The globalist's plans were to get rid of the family and masculinity so war wouldn't happen see.

APPEASEMENT NEVER WORKS

Appeasement [caving] is never how you deal with evil--they're still gonna rob, steal and kill.

It was the most extreme policies imaginable propounded in the most boring speech ever.

"America's Families Plan" is pure socialism veiled by euphemisms like the deceptive title ma'am.

Joe Biden's "Infrastructure" bill is nothing but a liberal wish list for big government waste.

Recap of his boring speech: open borders, defunding police and the largest pork bill in history.

Not one word on our Southern Border Crisis cuz Joe Biden IS the crisis since he INVITED it.

To save American families we're gonna grow government with "infrastructure", a misnomer.

You can't control a moral people, you gotta demoralize em and then you got em. JLPeterson

When you pay people to be poor you wind up with a lot of poor people. Milton Friedman

Why are they picking on Rudy? Republican, ran for president and friend of Donald Trump.

LIBERAL LOSERS

600,000 deaths in Civil War, only ONE in the capital riot and it was a Trumpster--but they're equal?

"REVISED CURRICULUMS"

"Revised curriculums": vacuous virtue signaling and regressive race-obsessed revisionism.

Lucky Chinese kids aren't learning "race politics" but real mathematics to their great success.

All this race stuff isn't coming from YOUR mind, you're just parroting them and it's so boring.

The loving liberals are violent. They put bombs in my mailbox, ruined my rep and they gossiped.

What the news denies is where the truth lies. But liberals are the opposite, conformists.

"If the Calif. recall wins it'll turn the state over to anti-mask, anti-vax pro-Trump extremists."

U.S. dumps the most banned vaccine in the world on India--it dissolves platelets/blood in ya.

RACIAL ESSENTIALISTS

Democrats are "racial essentialists" seeing all blacks without agency due to white supremacy.

They wanna teach indigenous history spanning back 1000 years not American like the frontiers.

Sequence of events: Berlin was the most debauched city in the 20's then later lost everything.

And so ANY black conservative is instantly pegged Uncle Tom, a cuckhold who has given in.

LIBERAL LOSERS

"The most devastatingly powerful speech we've ever heard." That's what they said/how absurd.

How did they conquer the west? Thru migrant invasions, viruses and closes businesses.

Not only the border crisis but AGAIN he's invited ISIS like what happened when he left Iraq.

No wonder they get nothing done in that culture and their mosques are built by foreigners.

The most reckless and divisive: saying the 1-6 capital march was equal to 911 or Pearl Harbor!

The Number One worst terror threat in America according to Biden is "white supremacy"

When a country is economically weakened it's sovereignty is open to challenge/e.g. Biden.

They're taught that the color of their skin defines them again--they're an "oppressor" if white skin.

HIX POLITIX

The ones least impacted by their bad bills are the ones controlling our fate and loss of life thrills.

All anti-discrimination legislation entails new forms of discrimination. Dr. Steve Turley

Liberty is a value, not a human instinct. Without instinct for liberty they just wanna be protected.

Modern man gives up his desire for LIBERTY cuz he wants big government to care for thee.

Without this natural desire for liberty we fall into tyranny very easily--we're one generation away see.

LIBERAL LOSERS

A handful value liberty but by far the most wanna be taken care of and that's how it takes off.

Republicans are the guardians of freedom in America while the left took over like with Obama.

MORE GUNS LESS CRIME

More guns equals less crime. It's never the opposite like the liberals are saying, that's a lie.

We love Pres. Trump and everything he stands for. He IS the party, we just have to adjust that's all.

Lady Gaga without evidence says Trumpsters took her two dogs tho' in crime-land Los Angeles.

This is what Martial. Law is: people can't leave their homes. God's on our side, just hold on.

It's one set of laws for the far left democrat socialists and another set of laws for the rest of us.

It's a dystopian barren land replete with poor relationship skills and Intimacy anorexia.

That faux pas you're ashamed of is just a foggy memory at best or even seen as genius.

Trauma brings moral and boundary-collapse: imagine that. In distress you face the world's slap.

Right when you're most traumatized evil flows in unobstructed and it's even worse guys.

The founders said low government was only possible with moral people or it's tyranny for all.

After the war is over and you're in safety try not to think about the war but just enjoy see.

ARNOLD EHRET FOREVER

Everything but fruits and veg creates acid, so if you're eating culture food it'll be pain I said.

Acid-reflux groups all over facebook but no one addresses the alkaline fruit issue?

Eat just fruit/greens and no acid-reflux. Eat anything else and the pain all night really sux.

Never trust restaurants with unvacuumed carpets and disorderly stations, they reflect kitchens.

The bloodstream is a water well circulating thru each cell so the whole skin system looks swell.

A wrinkled mess turns taut and shiny in three days as a fruit juice fast heals and rejuvenates.

ACID REFLUX is my reaction to everything wrong inner or outer. It's really my barometer.

Acid reflux is my barometer. I'm in insane pain day and night lest I heed what I'm saying here.

Greens seem fine, they go alkaline--but what about the oxalates, anti-nutrients and goitrogens?

Cure for all disease: see body as a sewer then clear all the veins so the new blood can heal ya'.

FOOD AND WHERE I'M AT NOW

It was a sad time when mental illness and malnutrition took over: there was so much depletion I acted out all over.

It all started with vegan hysteria. I was mentally ill until I added cheese now for my diet it's most of it.

LIBERAL LOSERS

I was also mentally ill from the SRI's they gave me in my twenties. The effects lasted over three decades.

SRIs are anti-depressants and anti-psychotics. The latter killed my brother in law.

My dad was a pharmacist, my brother a biochemist for a drug company and I rejected it all.

Minimalism is an adaptation--to keep just the quintessential--in order to maximally adapt.

If there's too much to think about—possessions, even those in storage--one can't do that.

We all have two lives. The second one starts when we realize we only have one. Tom Hiddleston

It's all stuff vs. experience. Are you a stuff person or an experience person? It's a budget regardless.

I don't think about lowcarb, highcarb, cooked or raw. I eat what I want but fast a long time in between--wow!

Some dried fruit or nuts in the afternoon if you get hungry. Stop making a big deal out of meals, you'll be happy.

HEALTH UPDATES

I've been pomegranate juice fasting for three days and WOW WOW WOW is all I gotta say.

The more you're into food [sex, booze, etc] the less you're into them and they react too.

Marriage was always seen as necessary protection for a woman but now not all of a sudden.

Why I don't respond: If too dumb to get it I'm not gonna waste a buncha words explaining it.

LIBERAL LOSERS

We say "I don't care what they think" while caring desperately what they think: how weak.

Just remember they hated Trump before they hated you. The dumbed hate anything new.

Let me get this straight. You can say what you want but not me? That's dumb responding to novelty.

For every sin there's a seed of compensation in the present moment, that's how they know it.

Loss of boundaries/downed hedges is torture on sensitives while invaded by dumbheads.

Never let em manhandle/pick up your cats under the guise of "petting"--that's just imposing.

ANOREXIA/FOOD OBSESSIONS

It's relieving knowing it's genetic--symptoms roll out with stress--but it's degrading nonetheless.

Food addiction takes one over like a consuming fire till you wanna eat the entire world I swear.

Bulimia is the Ugly Green Demon. It takes over personality till it's gone/empty inner realm.

The ugly green demon is a chipmunk face with panic in the eyes as he craves those French fries.

Eating disorder experts say bulimics are promiscuous kleptomaniacs, "side" symptoms I guess.

We went to a rally at a high school and used the lady's room and heard puking in the bathroom!

Why deny the bulimia of ancient Greece? They wanna make sin a disease not a party or relief.

LIBERAL LOSERS

After recovery we're just anorexogenic: emaculate housekeepers loving order like a lunatic.

It's about what it's like to be imposed on by people who are bigger or more socially "connected".

ANA is reclusive, spiritual, hypersensitive--in crowds prickly moods but evolves in solitude.

HAPPY WHEN I'M NOT EATING

I can't believe my acid reflux is gone. I just had to stop eating, that's all. Food is poison, that's all I know.

I'm only happy when I'm not eating. Sounds like mom near the end--she went into a fastarian world, dreamy.

Caution with "cashmere blend". It could have polyester in it or other deadly modern fabrics—lethal/sickening.

OK I won't call you a bad driver just a "European" driver but that doesn't make it any easier for me dear.

It took me a lifetime to prioritize black cashmere cardigan vests which for office/house warmth are the best.

Since I know God, I can't believe I'm gonna get sick and die early cuz I'm not eating a buncha meat. Agreed?

Many of the saints in monasteries lived on in-house bakery and wine. Veggies too but little if any swine.

American Christians had Sunday pot roast dinners after church. Christians were TWO [meat/not] types.

THE HUMAN OMNIVORE

Humans are omnivores—they can adapt to all diets—so the current carnivore craze is misleading to us.

LIBERAL LOSERS

You can eat all the meat you want, I won't judge you. But when it comes to what I eat I **JUST DON'T WANT TO.**

Chemicals create a dumbed down look: the thoroughbred height-width ratio of the skull is gone, it's a box now.

The aristocratic "T" scale is long and narrow but who has this now since we're all inundated with chemicals?

Third day on the fast and I'm just amazed. I feel so rejuvenated, healed of a trauma in recent days.

I will do a camouflaged fast the rest of the time: nursing fruit smoothies with mango, coconut, nut butter.

My acid reflux is **GONE!** Three decades of pain all day long. Have canceled my appointment for the doc.

My acid reflux came from trying to digest solid non-fruit foods. Just smoothies and Karen's Healthy Candy.

I feel so rejuvenated after my **TRAUMA,** the **FAST** and now I'm ensconced in holiday **SNOW.** It's a new day.

Addiction crosses a line and is inevitable. I've recalibrated the brain and now it's fasting I'm addicted to.

MINI-FASTING ROUTINE IN TRAUMA

Three days ago I was in an intense Trauma One. I stepped into a fast and now I've never been so high/in love.

I've got something now, a "Trump" card I always use. Go into a fast. While they eat, you're on top/just cruise.

Just a three day fast eliminated 30 years of acid reflux excruciating every day and night. What insight!

And I **CAN** live on fruit smoothies. I can't eat much else except twice a week digestive burn. Fast, restore it.

LIBERAL LOSERS

Mom's cancer from the grave: Thank you Karen for your blender meals, cuz I couldn't eat anything else."

Her daily one meal was avocado-tomato-lemon blended, mine is mango-coconut-nutbutter-healthy candy.

And to eliminate culture food desires? Have some pizza twice a week, to heck with it. No harm, we love it.

Some say "you must be an anorexic to talk like this". No, I'm anorexogenic/never bulimic, optimized by thinness.

After my fast I had a synchronistic and profound awakening to symbolic meaning--couldn't believe it.

Now life took on a profound sense of meaning--no time for B.S., no more time-wasting/wasters or imposers.

This way the kitchen stays clean and there's nothing in the fridge just my frozen fruit for the smoothie.

PIZZA DAY THEN BACK TO CORNUCOPIA

After my pizza on Saturday I go into one day fruit smoothie, next day total fast, next day fruit, next day pizza.

I have no more acid reflux eating this way, as the digestive fire really burns when it's so seldom.

I eat, then I don't eat. I look forward to the mini-fast then the mango smoothie tastes so good, then fauna.

I couldn't believe the miraculous discharge from the core after a mere 36 hour fast. A lifetime worth, alas.

I love the simplicity of all this cuz I eat just to get back to work, and I've witnessed the benefits of the fast.

Bread and butter for the long haul. Not lowfat highcarb--just bread--or highfat lowcarb--just the butter.

LIBERAL LOSERS

Pizza is a perfect breakfast no matter what they say. Buy 100 dough balls, freeze em and make it each day.

HEALTH UPDATES

Uncle died at 102, dad at 84, aunt at 91. I'm 71 and just now at my apex--coming into my own.

Smoothies, cliff bars, crackers/bread, grape juice/dates. Other than that no nightshades like spuds.

I'm not eating baguettes for nutrition but to push things down. There's nutritional vs. mechanical.

Breakfast is mechanical, lunch is more nutritional. Smoothies are best here to not choke.

Instead of fibbing to the authorities the two sisters created calumny by vicious gossip only.

When I think of a steak my mind congers the slaughterhouse and I don't see this changing now.

Age has made me harmless/gentle and my tender heart can't take that--I'll stick to dairy for my animal fat.

My new word for fasting: Eating Every Two Days. If anything a little mango juice in between pizzas.

How can this dynamo be seventy I heard someone say. Cuz the temporal lobe opened up to reveal eternity.

Multiple Chemical Sensitivities [MCS] is an autoimmune response as the body attacks itself.

When Big Tech merges with Big Pharma you will be banned for bashing vaccines in America.

END OF A LONG JOURNEY

LIBERAL LOSERS

"No Censorship" groups will just delete you to shut you up--mental tyranny is everywhere: duh.

But refuse stupid controversies with the ill-informed for they foster strife and breed quarrels.

As you mature intellectually you will use worthy debate not resort to insults or childish cults.

The lack of civility is enough to make a person isolate in his little cocoon for life see, like me.

You say anything against the narrative and they fight back with insults cuz that's all they have.

The public schools purposefully dumbed your kids down so now they're hell to be around.

I'm waiting to be led. Because when God pulls you it is irresistible and He takes you to The End.

Psychologists are clinicians or researchers but there's a tiny group called THEORETICIANS.

In any no-censorship group, prepare to be banned cuz that's the only way they stop you man.

AT THE TOP OF MY GAME

I'm at my highest pinnacle so stop saying I'm a relic cuz it's old paths we should restore quick.

Tho' we don't know the difference between illusion and truth we must carry on as if we do.

I wanted to go where there's nothing to do. Where no one wants to go but it's beautiful too.

To be a writer the point is to live not to write and when the Potter's done it explodes all day/night.

LIBERAL LOSERS

You gotta move with the spirit because if you wait you'll forget it. Do it **NOW** when you think of it.

Borders are open, their guilty conscience can rest but at a huge cost to the country and the west.

The goal is to reverse **ALL** Trump's decisions and the devastating results don't matter to them.

Sending Americans to die in faraway lands for unknowable gains, that's how they reign.

BULLY-PROOF IS HARD WORK

Becoming bully-proof was hard work, it started with my decision to take control but through words, that's all.

God isn't stupid, He doesn't need your longwinded prayers just intending to get attention from the others.

The work is my last chance to compete with youth before going into withering solitude which is so cool.

These books are my only legacy I'm leaving the earth. Like many of my relatives I was childless/God came first.

I won't state facts or stats or likely outcome of this, let's just let it take us to a new world of bliss.

Jesus saved me from the whole mess then after repentance He actually **ERASED** all of it.

Picturestrip: the more images in the set the less variation between each one so get enough KK said. www.karenkellock.org

BARREN LAND WITH NO LOVE

It's a dystopian barren land replete with poor relationship skills and intimacy anorexia.

LIBERAL LOSERS

That faux pas you're ashamed of is just a foggy memory at best or even seen as genius.

Trauma brings moral and boundary-collapse: imagine that. In distress you face the world's slap.

Right when you're most traumatized evil flows in unobstructed and it's even worse guys.

The founders said low government was only possible with moral people or it's tyranny for all.

After the war is over and you're in safety try not to think about the war but just enjoy see.

THE WAR WAS YOUR STEPPING STONE

The WAR was your stepping stone to victory and sheer enjoyment of this moment so forget it.

Don't wreck the present by ruminating what you went thru to get here, that's a waste friend.

You had to go thru THAT to get to HERE and it made you far greater/a biggor overcomer.

You had to go thru all THAT to realize the supromo importance of maintaining boundaries.

I had to be imposed on by a buncha dirty rats to stop letting em in and being a good hostess.

I was terrified to say NO. I had to be imposed on by grasping violent teens to become bold.

Why ruminate over sad lessons bringing you to victory in the present? Command: forget.

Now you live in a castle with a molt around it. How did you get it? Seeing the essentiality of it.

RECAP

You dodge the natives by learning about em. You simply turn your ship a notch then go on.

On top of the mountain you're all alone but stop hankering for old pillars/look up to God.

Why is luck the "residue of design"? It's the same as saying chance favors a prepared mind.

You portray yourself as a player but you ain't nothing but a **PAYER** you wicked whoremonger.

Stop seeking nurturance from old rejectors. It's a sign you're still sick so now explore the inner.

I'm a strong woman, hear me roar! That's the cry of weak conformists and nothing more.

Why keep going back if it's frustration and anger? This is not a good thing, stay **CENTERED.**

You're under His hand, hidden until you're not. Don't see it as rejection, it's the plan of God.

I'm a racist if I believe in immigration laws and a border. That's how crazy it is in this era.

If Hamas had no weapons there'd be peace. If Israel had no weapons they'd be **DESTROYED.**

The king on the mountain doesn't worry over rejection or disapproval by those on the bottom.

It wasn't ready then. It's all a matter of God's timing, not yours or mine. Wait for **YOUR TIME.**

If you cough every single time when taking a toke you **KNOW** you're not supposed to smoke.

100 KAREN KELLOCK BOOKS

AFFINITY OR MISERY
AGELESS CORNUCOPIA
AMERICA AWAKE!
AMERICA'S DAFT ERA
ARTS OF PALEO FASTING
AUTOPHAGY ON CHEATERS
BACKSTABBING NEUROTICS
BETRAYAL TRAUMA
BOOMERS AND BROKENNESS
BOOT ON NECK
CHAMPION GUIDES
COMMIE NUTHOUSE
COMMIES
COMMUNIST SPIRIT
CONTAGION OF MADNESS
CONTAGIOUS MADNESS
CULTURE CLASH BASHED
DAFT LEFT
DAILY FASTARIAN
DAM RATS
DIVERSITY IS CRUELTY
E-RACE WHITE
EVIL FREAKS (Beyond Gross)
THE END OR A BEND?
FEMALE BULLIES AND FEMI-NAZIS
FEMALE CARNALITY
FEMALE DUMB DOWN
FEMALE POWER DRIVE
FEMINISM AND RUIN 1 & 2
FIX FOR MISFITS
FOOLS & TRAMPS
FREEDOM SPEAKING
FRENEMY ENABLER
FRENEMY LIAR
FRENEMY THIEF
FRENEMY TRAITOR
TRENEMY TYRANT
GENIUS IS HELD DOWN
GLOBALISLAM
GOD USES THE FLAWED
HAZE OF THE LATTER DAYS

THE HERD IN WORDS
HIX POLITIX
HOW THEY RUINED US
JUST SKIP DINNER
LE FEMME AND THE COMMUNIST SPIRIT
LIBERAL CHAOS & ROT
LIBERAL DOUBLETHINK
LIBERAL GALL 1 & 2
LIBERAL SHOVE-DOWNS
LOCK YOUR GATE
LOSERS and Femme Fatales
MANUAL FOR SUPERIOR MEN
MODERN ART FROM HELL
MOSTLY FAKE
NOTES TO CHAMPS 1 & 2
OVERCOME FRENEMIES
PC MAKES US CRAZY
PEOPLE ARE CRUEL
PEOPLE PROBLEMS 1 & 2
PERSECUTED GENIUIS
POLI-PSYCH MYSTERIES
PRETENTIOUS SLOBS
QUEEN BEE
RED NEW DEAL
RETURNING TO FIRST NATURE
SEASON OF TREASON
SEPARATE MEANS HOLY
SOCIAL HYPNOTISM
SOLITUDE SOLUTION
SUPERCILIOUS
THE SCHOOLS SCREWED EM UP
TOAD TO PRINCE
TRIALS CYCLES
TRUMP VS. GROUP
TRUST IN TRASH
THE TRUTH ABOUT PEOPLE
UNDERHEANDEDLY CLEVER
WALK TALL WITHIN WALLS
WE'RE NOT ALL ONE
WINNERS SKIP DINNER
WORK OR SMERK

AUTHOR BIO
Karen Kellock Ph.D.

Ph.D Political Psychology, UCI 1976
Post-Doctoral: UCI Medical School
Department of Psychiatry
Grants NIMH, NIAAA

Ph.D. dissertation "A Systems-Theoretic View of Pathologic Interaction" made an early mark as the "Wife of the Alcoholic Syndrome". Postdoctoral research at UCI Medical, Dept. of Psychiatry on the systems surrounding pathology on NIMH and NIAAA federal grants: *The Contagion of Madness: The Psychology of Neurotic Interaction and Pathological Systems*. Therapy tool Therapeutic Playwriting introduced the play *Mary and Murv: Gruesome Twosomes in the Alcoholic Marriage*. She taught Abnormal Psychology and Pathological Systems Theory at UC and CSU campuses and developed "the Debris Theory of Disease" in five books and website: (www.karenkellock.org): *Champion Guides, Daily Fastarian, Just Skip Dinner, Arts of Paleo Fasting, Ageless Cornucopia. Manual for Superior Men is a* pick-it-up-anywhere book that you can't put down (20,000 Kellockialisms) and ever on your desktop it should be found (or this Ebook for superior wordsearch of new jargon).